MOUNTAIN BIKING TRAIL CENTRES THE GUIDE

TOM FENTON

MOUNTAIN BIKING TRAIL CENTRES THE GUIDE

TOM FENTON

VERTEBRATE **PUBLISHING**

Published by Vertebrate Publishing, Sheffield – www.**v-publishing**.co.uk

MOUNTAIN BIKING TRAIL CENTRES THE GUIDE

TOM FENTON

VERTEBRATE GRAPHICS

Copyright © 2008 **Vertebrate Graphics Limited**
(**www.v-graphics.co.uk**) and **Tom Fenton**.
Published by **Vertebrate Publishing** 2008.

ISBN: 978-1-906148-01-0

Front cover photo: Jonathan Campbell on the Red Route at
Dalby. Photo: Nick Hill.
Back cover photo: Glentress Red Route. Photo: Hamish McCool.
All other photographs as credited.

VERTEBRATE PUBLISHING

Designed and produced by Nathan Ryder –
Vertebrate Publishing, Sheffield.
www.**v-publishing**.co.uk

Acknowledgements

Researching and writing this book would have been a whole lot
harder without a bit of help. So, thank you to Fred Yong, Pete Dodd,
Rich Banyard, John Welford, Russ Walton, Ben Eagle, Pete Jenkins,
Andy Leviston, Pete Kenyon, Hazel Woodland, Sunit Pancholi,
Chris Arthur, Rik Alsop, Chipps, Guy Kesteven, Hugh Clixby,
Linus Naylor, the Forestry Commission and the various people
who answered questions or emails along the way. Thanks also
to Chris Fryer, Glen Saxton, Jon Lucas, Tim Russon and John
and Pat Horscroft.

Thanks also to all of the people who've supplied their photos:
Kitch and all the guys at MBR Magazine, Wig Worland
(*www.wigworland.com*), Dan Barham (*www.danbarham.com*),
Nick Hill (*www.nmdesign.co.uk*), Seb Rogers (*www.sebrogers.co.uk*),
Hamish McCool, Neill and Isobel at the Forestry Commission,
James Dymond, Paul Groom (*www.paulgroom.com*), Mark Pinder
(*www.thebppa.com/Mark-Pinder*), Pete Byrom, Dave Wilson,
Howard Cotton, John Coefield (*www.johncoefield.com*),
Tim Russon, Doug Inglis, Adam Titley, Mike Pruett, David Johnson,
David Smith, Chris Bartlett, Joanna Daxell, Scott Cramer and
Gary Williamson (*www.garywilliamson.co.uk*).

Finally, thanks to Peaty, Ian and the guys at Stif and Ibis and
the boys at Vertebrate for putting the book together –
Nathan and John.

**For information about trail centre updates and to download SatNav Point of
Interest files for free, please visit: www.ukmountainbiking.co.uk**

CONTENTS

Foreword

I'm a born and bred Yorkshire lad so obviously I favour my local forest as the best spot to ride in the UK: Wharncliffe has awesome technical trails which I believe have helped me become so good at what I do for a living.

But that's not all this book's about. There are dozens of trail centres popping up all over the UK and I have been lucky enough to ride quite a few of them. The UK has a passion for mountain biking like no other place I know and I think this is shown in the British team's regular successes at World Championships and World Cups; month after month and year after year our riders come up with the goods.

A lot of this passion for riding comes out in the trail centres we have too. The manmade parts are fun and flowing and keep everyone on their toes, there's the sweet singletrack that weaves along, or you can hop into the woods and dodge your way through trees and roots. Depending on your style you can go hard or just cruise, but either way you will get lots of enjoyment out of our Great British mountain biking trail centres.

We truly have something for everyone. Enjoy your ride.

Steve Peat
3x World Cup Mountain Bike Downhill Champion

STEVE PEAT COMPETING AT FORT WILLIAM 📷 JOHN COEFIELD

TOM FENTON AT GRIZEDALE 📷 JOHN COEFIELD

Introduction

Everybody likes singletrack.

Even if you're just starting out in biking and don't know what singletrack is, trust us – you'll like it. We certainly do.

Unless you know an area particularly well, the easiest way to guarantee a singletrack-packed ride is to head to one of the many excellent trail centres around the UK. But which one? Which will you enjoy the most? Is it easy/hard enough? How will you get there? Is there a café? Does it cost to ride?

We've created this guide to answer these questions. We went out and rode at every trail centre in the country in order to give you an unbiased view on exactly what you'll find at each one. We've listed their trails, their facilities; we've stuck in some directions and added any other snippets of information we think might help you plan a trip.

We've concentrated on cross-country trails, because everybody rides them, but have included downhill runs where they appear alongside XC trails at mountain bike centres. So, whether you're a complete beginner or are out riding daily, this guide will help you plan your trail centre trips.

Have fun!

Tom Fenton

About trail centres

Way back in the early 1990s, mountain bikers Sian and Dafydd Roberts had the idea of creating a dedicated, mountain bike-only trail. They were running Coed y Brenin's visitor centre café at the time and wanted to loop the trail through the woods there. They approached the Forestry Commission, which liked what it heard and brought in one of its employees, Dafydd Davis, to design and build what, in 1997, became the Red Bull trail.

This purpose-built, waymarked trail was a world first and a massive success. Mountain bikers rushed to Wales, visitor numbers to the area went through the roof and it wasn't long before the Forestry Commission wanted more. Trails popped up all over Wales and then spread out into Scotland and England, and things are looking promising in Ireland. Private landowners also got in on the act. Now, there are over 60 hugely popular trail centres across the UK and riders make massive trips across the length and breadth of the country to ride them.

It's easy to see why the trails have become so popular. A good ride is guaranteed, no matter what the weather. The manmade nature of the trails has created a new style of riding, with bermed corners, smooth jumps and flowing singletrack – not things found so easily or so often on natural trails. Clear waymarking has removed the need for a map, for navigational skills and for route planning. Beginners can turn up, knowing they'll be able to ride a trail at their level, while advanced riders are assured of a good, technical ride. Essentially, a trip to a trail centre minimises stress and maximises fun.

But is this a good thing? Have trail centres removed the adventure from mountain biking? Do you really want to visit North Wales and spend all your time riding in a forest that's similar to one in South Wales? Where's the fun in heading out along a trail knowing for sure that everything you encounter was designed to be, and can be, ridden? Aren't 'natural' trails better after all?

As with everything, the answer lies somewhere in the middle. Trail centre riding might have taken some of the 'soul' out of mountain biking... but it always offers an amazing ride in return – and you can't really argue with that!

COED Y BRENIN 📷 HAMISH McCOOL

How to use this book

➊ Beginners/Intermediate/Advanced

These give an idea of how *suitable* a centre is for riders of different abilities, not how enjoyable the riding will be. We have rated the suitability on a scale of '**0**' to '**3**'. A '**0**' means there's nothing for a particular group, a '**1**' suggests a trail that could be ridden, but which isn't ideal. A '**2**' suggests suitable, but limited riding whereas a '**3**' means there's loads to go at. The rating does not take into account the style of riding. A rating of '**3**' for advanced riders could indicate the presence of a highly technical north shore trail, or a very long ride requiring a good level of fitness.

- A **beginner** is taken to be someone who rides **green/blue** trails.
- **Intermediate** riders enjoy **red** trails.
- **Advanced** riders will prefer **black** and **orange**-graded riding.

A beginners' rating of '**1**' suggests that a confident and fit beginner *might* be able to ride at a centre, not that they *will* be – look at the individual centre listing and make your own decision. A degree of subjectivity is employed, as, for example a good rider will always get round an easy trail, although they may find it boring. The rating attempts to reflect this.

➋ Facilities

A list of centre facilities (see Key). Only centres which have no waymarked trail riding have the 'No Trail Markers' symbol. All other centres feature at least one waymarked trail.

➌ The trails

Name, grade and distance of trail.

➍ Nearest bike shop

As it suggests…

WHINLATTER FOREST

➊ **AT A GLANCE**
BEGINNERS: 1/3   INTERMEDIATE: 3/3   ADVANCED: 2/3

➋ **FACILITIES**

➌ **THE TRAILS**
Altura Trail .... Red 16km

➍ **NEAREST BIKE SHOP**
Cyclewise (on site) – t: 01768 778 711
Keswick Mountain Bikes, Keswick – t: 01768 780 586

➎ **MORE INFORMATION**
w: www.forestry.gov.uk

About the centre

➏ ...ing to the west of Keswick in the northern Lake District, Whinlatter Forest is a great spot. An attractive, steeply-sided forest, it boasts some great views out over Bassenthwaite Lake and the surrounding area. It also contains the Altura Trail, a figure of eight loop built by Clixbys trail builders and running to the north and south of the main visitor centre.

Centre pros and cons

➐ ...olid singletrack trail
...reat location
+ Lots more planned!

Directions

➑ ...a Keswick, take the A66 west towards Cockermouth. ...r a couple of miles, enter the village of Braithwaite and immediately turn left onto the B5292. Follow the road through the village and up into Whinlatter Forest. The car park and visitor centre will be on your right.
Grid Ref: NY 209245   **Sat Nav:** CA12 5TW

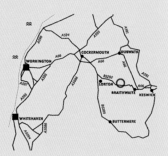

FACILITIES KEY

- 🚲 – Bike Hire
- 🔧 – Bike Shop
- 💧 – Bike Wash
- ☕ – Café
- ⛺ – Campsite

- 🛏 – Other Accommodation
- Ⓟ – Pay & Display
- 🏛 – Place of Interest
- 🚉 – Rail Link
- 📷 – Scenic
- 🛒 – Shop

- 🚿 – Showers
- 🚻 – Toilets
- 🔄 – No Trail Markers
- ⬆ – Uplift Service
- ℹ – Visitor Centre
- Ⓨ – Youth Hostel

The Trails

ALTURA TRAIL		**9**
DISTANCE: 16KM	**TIME:** 1–2HRS	
EFFORT: 3/5	**TECHNICALITY:** 3/5	**10**

Taken steadily, the relatively straightforward Altura Trail makes a pleasant ride. The woodland is pretty, the birds are probably singing and there are some great views to admire from the climbs. Hit with a bit more speed, the trail takes on a completely different character. Try not to touch the brakes through the flowing corners, big berms and jumps and you can add a massive dose of fun to the experience. Although relatively straightforward, this trail isn't a pushover – the climbs have some tight corners and there are a few sharp climbs, rocks and roots that might catch out the unwary. A great trail – fun for relatively inexperienced riders and fast riders alike.

JOHN COEFIELD

JOHN COEFIELD

5 More information
Useful websites and contact information.

6 About the centre
General introduction to each trail centre.

7 Centre pros and cons
A list of pros and cons for each centre.

8 Directions
From the nearest large town or major road. OS grid references for luddites and postcodes for Sat Navs. Where we haven't been able to establish an accurate postcode we've given the name of the nearest town.

The trails
9 Colour grades
Forestry Commission trail gradings. *See page 12.*

10 Effort/Technicality
When is a red trail not a red? These ratings give an idea of the effort and level of technical difficulty of a trail:

Effort
1 = A short ride with no major hills, suitable for most riders, including children.

3 = Getting longer and/or hillier. If you're pretty fit, or ride fairly regularly, you'll be fine here.

5 = A long, or hilly ride. You'll need to ride hard on a regular basis to enjoy these routes.

Technicality
1 = Flat trails, nothing tricky – your Gran could get around these.

3 = Plenty of twisty singletrack with a light dusting of rocks and roots. Tricky in places, but nothing terrifying.

5 = Rocks, roots, steep drops, jumps. Crashing almost guaranteed for all but the very best.

Forestry Commission grading system

Green (Easy)

If you're healthy, you should be fine on a green trail with a basic mountain bike or hybrid. Expect relatively flat and wide trails with the odd stretch of singletrack and occasional loose/muddy sections, but no technical obstacles or steep gradients.

Blue (Moderate)

If you've got basic off-road skills, are reasonably fit and own a basic mountain bike, you'll be fine. There will be more singletrack, rocks and roots than a green trail; the riding will be technically more difficult and probably a little bit steeper (going up **and** coming back down).

Red (Difficult)

You'll need to have decent riding skills, be fit and ride a 'proper' mountain bike for a red trail. There will be a lot of singletrack, with variable surfaces and tricky obstacles. Trails will be technical with features such as berms, steps, boardwalk, drops and off-camber sections.

Black (Severe)

Suitable for technically very able riders who are used to physically demanding riding over an extended period of time. Trails will be hard, with long sections of singletrack, large and committing obstacles, and sections of unrelenting technicality. Expect to find harder versions of all the technical features of a red trail.

Orange (Bike Parks, Extreme)

Good fitness will help, but a very high level of technical ability is essential, as is an appropriate bike. Expect very challenging riding with large, unavoidable obstacles, steep gradients and high levels of exposure and risk. Trails will vary from jumps and north shore to full-on downhilling. Jumping is often compulsory.

Purple (Ungraded)

The odd trail in this book hasn't been given a grade. In some cases, this is because the FC hasn't graded them. In others, such as Swinley Forest, this is because the forest is full of singletrack that you can mix and match to create your own route. If there's no grade, check the 'effort' and 'technicality' ratings and the accompanying text.

Pay attention to grades and warning signs – they are there for a reason. Be honest about your riding abilities and use appropriate equipment, but don't be too put off by grades, deciding that something is too hard for you even before you've seen it. Mountain biking began with people fitting fat tyres to their bikes and discovering what was rideable. Maps rarely grade trails and we've never seen a sign in the middle of the Peak District warning that the bridleway ahead is a 'Red Descent with Double Black options'. Essentially, use some common sense and be realistic about what you attempt, but remember that you'll never become a better rider if you don't try.

Which bike shall I take?

There is no 'best bike' for trail centre riding. For green routes, virtually any bike will work, although a mountain bike is probably the safest bet, especially for somewhere like Brechfa. For the XC-style loops, virtually any half-decent mountain bike will be a lot of fun. Lightweight hardtails are fun to flick through tight singletrack, while full-suspension bikes tend to be more comfortable and faster. If you're heading for downhill runs, jumps or bike parks, pick something tough that's designed for the job.

Check everything's working – especially for harder riding. You won't be going uphill fast if your gears seize but may be quicker than planned downhill if your brakes don't work. Pump the tyres up, check that nothing's about to fall off or wear through and check that everything that should be tight is tight.

What shall I stick in my bag?

Food and water. Ideally, you want to be drinking around half a litre of water for every hour of exercise. Any less and your performance – and therefore your enjoyment – may start to suffer. If you're on a long ride, high-carbohydrate foods, such as bananas and cereal bars, will keep you going for longer.

A **multi-tool** (with a chain breaker), a **spare tube** or two and a **pump**, along with any specific spares your bike needs. A mechanical problem miles from home is no fun.

Waterproofs, a **first aid kit** and **spare clothing** could all come in handy. What would happen if you fell off miles from home, in a rainstorm and had to wait for help? A relevant **map** is worth having, as is a **mobile phone**, although you can't always rely on getting a signal.

Sorted clothing will help you stay comfortable on your bike, especially in bad weather. The layering system is the easiest way to do this, as you can remove/add layers as conditions change. Wear 'technical' synthetic or wool fabrics next to your skin to move moisture away from your body. (Stay away from cotton – it absorbs moisture and holds onto it, causing chafing and making you cold.) If it's chilly, an insulating layer over this will keep you warm and, on the outside, a windproof or waterproof layer will stave off the elements. Set off a little on the cool side – you'll soon warm up and won't have to stop to change – but don't leave your warm clothes behind in dodgy conditions, as the weather could turn.

Padded shorts are more comfortable, but the amount of lycra on display is entirely up to you. Baggy shorts, tights and trousers are all available for the hairy-legged.

Riding safely

Guess what – wear a **helmet**. And as *"the best helmet is the one that you're wearing"*, make sure it fits and is comfortable. Do it up correctly (so it doesn't move) and you're good to go.

Gloves might not seem to do much, but they are an easy way to avoid blisters and palms full of gravel.

Knee/shin, **elbow** and **spine protectors** are all available to help keep you intact and are highly recommended for downhill runs and bike parks – but they can be restrictive and uncomfortable. The same goes for **full-face helmets** – the greater protection will help keep your good looks, but they're hot and heavy. Think about where and what you're riding and choose accordingly.

Even though you might be on a one-way trail with *No Entry to Walkers* signs, it's worth keeping an eye on your speed. Just around that corner might be someone picking themselves up from a crash, a walker who's ignored the signs or somebody who thinks that taking a dog out for a ride is a good idea.

Trail centres can be great places to push yourself. There are plenty of technical features and jumps begging to be ridden. By all means go for it – you won't get better if you don't try, but be sensible about it and recognise your limits.

The fact that you're on a waymarked trail doesn't mean you're safe. Frames, parts and helmets can still be broken and the ground's as hard as anywhere else: we know of somebody who didn't even manage to make it out of Kirroughtree car park before concussing himself… Would you know the quickest way back to the car in the event of an accident? At the very least, pick up a trail map. Better still, pack a first aid kit and know how to use it.

If it all does go horribly wrong and you can't sort yourself out, call 999 and ask for POLICE – MOUNTAIN RESCUE.

A few thoughts on trail centre riding

If you're caught up by a faster rider, pull over when **you** are ready and let them pass. You don't want them pressuring you (riders behind you always sound closer than they actually are), they don't want to be stuck behind you and you'll both have more fun as a result.

On a similar note, **if you catch a slower rider**, don't get too close. You'll be making more noise than you realise and they'll think you're much faster and closer to them than you actually are, which could make them feel pressured – and that's not great. Either ask politely if you can nip past, hang back a bit and cruise or stop and let a gap open up.

Think about where you stop. Trail exits, blind corners and underneath jumps are **not** good choices. Don't push/ride back up trails, and get out of the way if you're fixing a bike.

Don't ride off the edges of the trail. You came here to ride the **single**track, right? So why would you want to make it wider? Equally – don't cut corners. What's the point? If you want to go somewhere and ride in a straight line, buy a road bike.

Rules of the (off) road

- Expect the unexpected – ride in control
- Remember other vehicles use forest roads as well as you
- Ride considerately – give way to horses and walkers
- Keep away from forest operations and closed-off trails
- Do not pass any vehicle loading timber until you have been told you may do so
- Leave no trace – take home everything you took out

AFAN ARGOED WIG WORLAND

OVERVIEW MAP

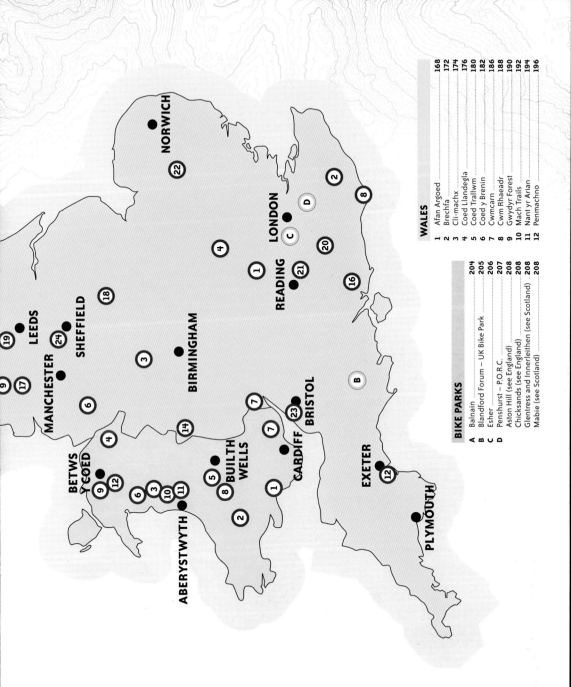

SECTION
ENGLAND

ASTON HILL

About the centre

Aston Hill has long been one of the south east's main downhill venues, having several tracks and a 4X course. In addition, it has a short, but fun singletrack XC loop. In the summer, the trails are rock solid, smooth and lightning-fast, whilst in the winter, the polished roots and slippery chalk take on ice-rink-like qualities. A popular venue amongst experienced riders, there's nothing for complete beginners, although the XC loop isn't too tricky. The hill regularly plays host to races, events and training sessions and has limited opening hours, so you'll need to check *www.rideastonhill.co.uk* for times and details if you're planning a visit.

Centre pros and cons

+ Short, but technical and entertaining XC loop
+ Aston Hill is one of the south east's best downhill venues, with several runs to choose from
+ Good 4X course
– Pay to ride (but free parking)
– Restricted opening
– No facilities

Directions

From Aylesbury, take the A41 south towards Hemel Hempstead. Follow the road as it becomes dual carriageway and then take the second exit onto the B4009. Follow this west towards Wendover, turning left to stay on the B4009. Once the woods appear on your left, turn left to climb a minor road. The car park is on your left about halfway up the hill.

Grid Ref: SP 891101   **Sat Nav:** HP22 5NQ

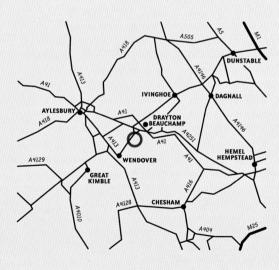

The trails

XC LOOP	
DISTANCE: c.9KM	**TIME:** 1–2HRS
EFFORT: 3/5	**TECHNICALITY:** 3/5

DOWNHILL AND 4X	
DISTANCE: N/A	**TIME:** N/A
EFFORT: 2/5	**TECHNICALITY:** 5/5

Aston Hill's XC loop is best ridden on a dry, sunny day when the trails are baked hard and fast. It combines a run down the easiest of the downhill trails with a leg-burning slog back to the top. The descent is a brilliant combination of high-speed, rooty straights and steep switchbacks. The climb is technically easy, but seriously steep and tough going. In winter, however, the polished roots and chalky singletrack become treacherously slick and it requires a fair degree of skill to stay upright! The trail is on the short side, but more than makes up in fun what it lacks in length.

There are four downhill tracks here, from the relatively smooth and easy Red Run that forms part of the XC course to the infamous Black Run, with its jumps, drops and tricky turns. The tracks all share two main features – they are steep and they are rooty. The 4X track, meanwhile, is much smoother and wider with a range of jumps and fast turns. Aston Hill may not have the size and length of some of the Welsh and Scottish venues, but it makes good use of what it has to produce some decent, fun tracks.

WIG WORLAND

BEDGEBURY

AT A GLANCE
BEGINNERS 2/3   INTERMEDIATE 3/3   ADVANCED 2/3

FACILITIES

THE TRAILS
Singletrack Trail .... Red 15km
Freeride Area .... Orange .... N/A
Family Trail .... Green 9km

NEAREST BIKE SHOP
Quench Cycles – t: 01580 879 694

MORE INFORMATION
w: www.forestry.gov.uk/bedgebury
Bedgebury Visitor Centre – t: 01580 879 820

About the centre

Bedgebury Forest is a 2000-acre forest in Kent. Managed by
the Forestry Commission, it's a popular and busy place, with a
Pinetum (lots of pine trees), a Go Ape course and other family
attractions. It has also, thanks to the FC and to Bedgebury Forest
Cycling Club, a 15km singletrack trail, a freeride area with north
shore and dirt jumps, and plenty of riding for families.
The singletrack is typical of that found in most areas of
woodland in the south east – fast, twisting and fun in the
summer, but muddy and hard work in winter.

Centre pros and cons

+ Lots of natural-feeling singletrack with good flow
+ North shore area surprisingly technical
+ Dirt jumps good for beginners
− Can get VERY muddy
− Very expensive to park at £7.50 at the time of writing
− No hills means lots of pedalling and no standout descents
− Nothing particularly technical – but that's the nature of the
  riding in the South East

Directions

From Royal Tunbridge Wells, follow the A21 south towards
Hastings. After about 9 miles, turn left onto the B2079 and
follow signs for Bedgebury.
Grid Ref: TQ 715332   **Sat Nav:** TN17 2SJ

The trails

SINGLETRACK TRAIL

DISTANCE: 15KM	TIME: 1–2.5HRS
EFFORT: 3/5	TECHNICALITY: 2/5

Imaginatively called the 'Singletrack' Trail, this is a pure XC trail that twists and turns through the woods. Although there are no major climbs or descents, there are enough changes in gradient to keep you interested, with a couple of steep-ish climbs and some entertaining descents. There's a fair percentage of singletrack, with trail surfaces varying from fast hardpack to dirt (which becomes thick mud in the winter). No big jumps or bermed sections, but plenty of roots and turns. Good, flowing cross-country fun.

Other riding

FREERIDE AREA

DISTANCE: N/A	TIME: N/A
EFFORT: 1/5	TECHNICALITY: 5/5

FAMILY TRAIL

DISTANCE: 9KM	TIME: 1–1.5HRS
EFFORT: 1/5	TECHNICALITY: 1/5

Bedgebury also boasts freeride and skills areas and a family trail. The freeride area contains some well-spaced small jumps – good for learning on as there's plenty of time to compose yourself between them – and some relatively extensive north shore. It's not too skinny or high, but tricky in places with drops, some interesting seesaw action and some big wooden berms. It gets pretty slick in the wet, so be warned. The skills area has a couple of planks to balance along, some logs to hop and some stumps to weave between. The family trail is on wide tracks with a very good surface, making it easy and well suited to children.

FORESTRY COMMISSION PICTURE LIBRARY / ISOBEL CAMERON

FORESTRY COMMISSION PICTURE LIBRARY / ISOBEL CAMERON

CANNOCK CHASE

About the centre

Right in the middle of England, Cannock Chase's Follow the Dog Trail can be easily reached by a lot of riders. Unsurprisingly, this had led to the trail taking a bit of a hammering, leading to heavy erosion. However, recent work by Chase Trails, the volunteer group who built and maintain the trails has significantly improved the trail, eliminating the bottomless pits of stinking black mud and introducing some sections of tight, narrow and twisting trail. As a result, this short route now boasts an enjoyable variety of singletrack and is great fun for a quick lap or two.

Centre pros and cons

+ Nice variety along the trail – there are tight bits, natural bits, surfaced bits…
+ Reasonably extensive set of DH runs
− Only the one XC trail
− Used to get very muddy, although this seems to have been resolved

Directions

The XC trails begin from the Birches Valley Visitor Centre, near Rugeley. In Rugeley, pick up the A51 from the roundabout where it joins the A460 and head north towards Wolseley Bridge. At the first set of traffic lights, turn left onto Hagley Road and follow this out of town. After a mile or so, turn left by the large Birches Valley sign, and then left again into the car park. Directions to the downhill area can be found opposite.

Grid Ref: SK 018170   **Sat Nav:** WS15 2UQ

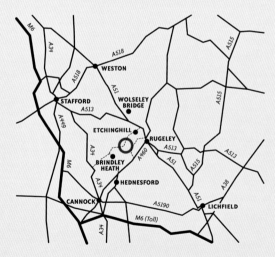

The trails

FOLLOW THE DOG	
DISTANCE: 11KM	**TIME:** 0.75–1.5HRS
TECHNICALITY: 3/5	**EFFORT:** 3/5

Mainly singletrack, and varied singletrack at that, this great little route is rideable in under an hour, yet is entertaining enough for repeat laps. Straight off the bat, you're twisting between pines on fast, tight, narrow singletrack. After a couple of short climbs the trail takes on a natural feel, winding through open woods and then dropping around a series of berms. There's a fast stony descent in a shallow gully, a loose climb and a high-speed open section – all good fun. Back into the woods, the trail throws in some awkward corners to keep you on your toes and squeezes through impossibly tight woodland (watch those bars) before opening out just enough to allow a bit of speed around the final corners.

DOWNHILL AREA	
DISTANCE: N/A	**TIME:** N/A
EFFORT: N/A	**TECHNICALITY:** 5/5

There are several downhill runs on Cannock Chase at Stile Cop near Rugeley. As the area isn't exactly mountainous, the runs are relatively short, taking perhaps a minute or so from top to bottom. They are fairly manmade in nature, containing a lot of berms, drops and jumps – some of which are fairly big, so you'd be wise to check them out first. To find the trails, leave Rugeley on the A460 heading for Hednesford and turn left just outside the town, following signs for the Cemetery. The car park is on the left at the top of the hill (**Grid Ref: SK 039151**) and the trails are on the other side of the road.

Good to know

There are other, more family-orientated trails on Cannock Chase, including a couple of green-graded forest road routes beginning near the Follow the Dog trail.

FORESTRY COMMISSION PICTURE LIBRARY

CHICKSANDS

AT A GLANCE
BEGINNERS: 2/3   INTERMEDIATE: 2/3   ADVANCED: 3/3

FACILITIES
(P)

THE TRAILS
Blue Route . . . . Blue 4km
Red Route . . . . Red 5.5km
Downhill / 4X / North shore . . . . Orange . . . . N/A

NEAREST BIKE SHOP
Pedals, Biggleswade – t: 01767 313 418

MORE INFORMATION
w: www.chicksandsbikepark.co.uk

Centre pros and cons

+ Extensive north shore with various lines
+ One of the better 4X courses in the area
− Not much for cross country riders

Directions

From Bedford, head south on the A600, following signs to
Shefford. Chicksands is in Rowney Warren Woods, which are
on your left after about 7.5 miles.

Grid Ref: TL 116416   **Sat Nav:** CHICKSANDS

About the centre

More for the jumpers and north shore riders than for XC guys,
Chicksands, or more accurately Rowney Warren, is a small area
of woodland near Bedford that's become a massively popular
riding spot. There are two XC trails – one for beginners and a
more advanced trail – an extensive set of north shore trails and
a range of dirt jumps and downhill runs. The XC trails are free,
but you need to pay to use the jumps and north shore stuff if
you're there at weekends.

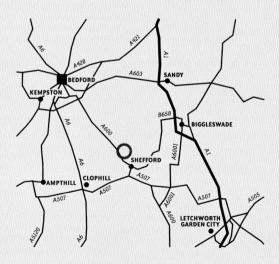

The trails

BLUE ROUTE	
DISTANCE: 4KM	**TIME:** 0.5–1HR
EFFORT: 1/5	**TECHNICALITY:** 1/5

RED ROUTE	
DISTANCE: 5.5KM	**TIME:** 0.5–1HR
EFFORT: 2/5	**TECHNICALITY:** 2/5

There are two trails here, a 4 km blue route and a 5.5km red route. The blue route sticks to wide forest trails and easy tracks and, although it can get muddy in winter, is very beginner-friendly. The red route, meanwhile, uses some of the forest's singletrack trails and steeper climbs to create a slightly more challenging route through the forest. Neither is particularly exciting for more experienced riders, although the red can be extended to take in some of the easier sections of the downhill/dirt jumps area if you're looking for something more challenging.

DOWNHILL / 4X / NORTH SHORE	
DISTANCE: N/A	**TIME:** N/A
EFFORT: N/A	**TECHNICALITY:** 5/5

You'll find more exciting riding up at the top (north) end of Rowney Warren. With a 4X course, a couple of sets of dirt jumps and drops of various shapes and sizes, there's plenty for jumpers and downhillers to go at. A little further into the woods is the freeride 'Chick Shore' area, with various north shore lines, gap jumps and drops. You need to pay to use this area at weekends and on bank holidays, and will be asked to wear a helmet at all times. See ***www.chicksandsbikepark.co.uk*** for more information.

ANDY CLARKE

DALBY

Centre pros and cons
+ Wide range of trails
+ Long red route with plenty of singletrack and shortcut options
+ Black route has a good mix of natural and manmade trails
- Expensive to get in
- Can get muddy

Directions
From Pickering, follow the A169 north towards Whitby, turning right just before the Fox and Rabbit Pub onto the Thornton-le-Dale road. The Forest Drive is on your left after a short way.
Grid Ref: SE 857873   **Sat Nav:** YO18 7LT

About the centre
As England's largest trail centre, Dalby Forest offers a wide range of trails, from very short, easy beginner routes to a 37km long singletrack red and the highly technical black route. The easier trails stick to forest roads, while the red contains a massive amount of singletrack and the black mixes up natural and manmade trails, making this a centre with something for everybody. Up at the higher car park is the Dixon's Hollow Bike Park with its jumps and north shore. To cap it off, there's also a full range of facilities, with a decent café and well-stocked bike shop on site.

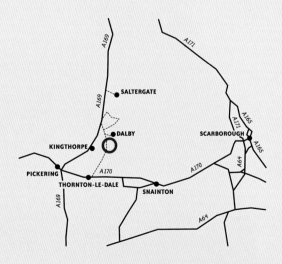

The trails

BLUE ROUTE

DISTANCE: 14KM	TIME: 1–2.5HRS
EFFORT: 2/5	TECHNICALITY: 2/5

Starting from the visitor centre car park, Dalby's blue route shares its initial singletrack climb with the red route. There are a few tight-ish corners and it's relatively steep in places – not too technical, but not a walk in the park. The route then follows forest routes for the remainder of its length, climbing gently at first and then descending quickly, back to the visitor centre. A good route for getting out and covering a fair distance, but not one for admiring the views or for swooping along singletrack.

RED ROUTE

DISTANCE: 37KM	TIME: 3–4HRS
EFFORT: 4/5	TECHNICALITY: 3/5

Dalby's red route is long. Although you can start it from either the upper or lower car parks, the latter is a better option as it means you finish off on a couple of good stretches of singletrack descent. There's a fair amount of singletrack on the route and although it's not massively technical or steep, it can be tiring, so several shortcuts have been signposted. The singletrack is nicely mixed, with some smooth sections through the woods, a few rocky stretches and plenty of roots here and there. There are fast, bermed descents, technically interesting climbs and lovely sweeping woodland trails. In short, a long route with a high proportion of good, varied singletrack.

Trails continue...

NICK HILL

DALBY
continued...

BLACK ROUTE

DISTANCE: 10KM	TIME: 1–2.5HRS
EFFORT: 3/5	TECHNICALITY: 4/5

Mixing tight, fast berms with rocky gullies, Dalby's Black Route demands a complete set of riding skills in order to be ridden well. Fast trails with jumps, tight berms through the woods and steep rocky descents test descending abilities while, on the way back up, you'll need fitness, stamina and technical climbing skills to complete the route cleanly. There's a north shore trail at crazy angles along a bramble-filled ditch, a rooty 'ridge' that's tricky to ride and some great, if more conventional, singletrack. Mixing manmade and natural terrain, this is a good ride.

Other riding

Dalby Forest has two green-graded trails, the **Ellersway Family Cycle Route**, beginning from the lower car park at Dalby Visitor Centre, and the **Adderstone Cycle Trail**, which starts further up the Forest Drive at Dixon's Hollow Car Park. The Ellersway Family Cycle Route is a 3km loop near the river on wide, flat trails whereas the Adderstone Cycle Trail traces a 10km route around higher ground, although it's still on wide trails and there's little climbing. The **Pace Bike Park** at Dixon's Hollow is a complete contrast, with a decent array of jumps and some reasonably extensive north shore – it's well worth a play for a couple of hours.

NICK HILL

DELAMERE

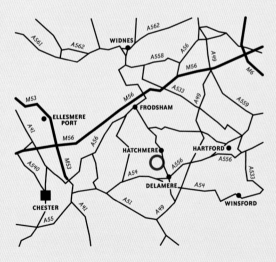
Centre pros and cons

+ Easy, waymarked trails are great for families
+ Fairly extensive skills area
+ Lots of singletrack (if you're prepared to explore)
– Skills area limited if you don't like to jump
– No waymarked singletrack

Directions

From Chester, take the A51 east towards Nantwich, turning left after 5 miles onto the A54, following signs to Manchester. After another 4 miles, turn left onto the A556 and then, once in Delamere, turn left onto the B5152. The visitor centre is on your left, by Delamere train station.

Grid Ref: SJ 548704   **Sat Nav:** CW8 2JD

About the centre

There's something for most riders in Delamere Forest. For families and beginners, there are two waymarked routes on easy tracks. For XC riders, there's plenty of singletrack weaving through the forest. For downhillers and jumpers, there's the cycle skills area with its jumps, 4X track and bermed runs. If you've ever watched the DVD *Earthed 3* and wondered where the Nigel Page and Steve Peat section was filmed, look no further. Easily reachable from Manchester, the forest is a popular spot with many, very different, riders.

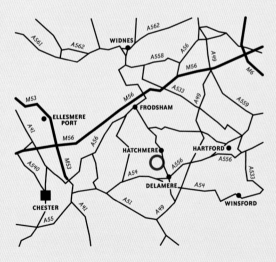

The trails

HUNGER HILL TRAIL	
DISTANCE: 6KM	**TIME:** 0.5–1.5HRS
EFFORT: 1/5	**TECHNICALITY:** 1/5

WHITEMOOR TRAIL	
DISTANCE: 11KM	**TIME:** 1–3HRS
EFFORT: 2/5	**TECHNICALITY:** 1/5

Two easy-riding trails run through Delamere Forest. Starting from the Linmere visitor centre, you have the choice of either following purple waymarks, which will take you around the 6km Hunger Hill Trail, or white arrows for the longer, 11km Whitemoor Trail. Both trails stick to well-surfaced and wide forest tracks and are ideal for family rides. Mountain bikers looking for singletrack might find the trails lack stimulation, but they offer a pleasant and easy way of exploring the forest.

SKILLS AREA AND SINGLETRACK	
DISTANCE: N/A	**TIME:** N/A
EFFORT: N/A	**TECHNICALITY:** N/A

Singletrack first; it's not waymarked or mapped, but there's dirt singletrack all over the forest. It's not particularly technical, but there's some good riding to be had. It's twisty and rooty enough to be interesting and with enough hills to be lively. Spin out from the visitor centre towards the skills area until you see something you like the look of. There is a decent-sized, dedicated cycle skills area with a 4X track, dirt jumps of various sizes, a few road (track) gaps and some short, bermed runs. Good fun, but a bit limited if you don't like your wheels in the air.

Good to know

To find the skills area, leave the visitor centre and turn left up the B5152. Turn left at the crossroads and the trails are on your right after about 2 miles (**Grid Ref: SJ 534716**). If you reach the railway bridge, you've gone too far. Layby parking is available.

CHRIS BARTLETT

FOREST OF DEAN

About the centre

Lying on the Wales/England border, the Forest of Dean is full of good mountain biking. There are wide forest tracks and there are sections of tight singletrack – all good fun. The FODCA Trail is the only waymarked singletrack loop in the forest, offering five kilometres of technical singletrack. It's not surfaced, which means it gets a little muddy in winter, but which also means that the trail is full of roots. If you can't and don't want to ride them then go elsewhere. If you can't ride them but want to learn, then this is the place. If you can ride them then you'll love hunting out the best lines through the trees!

Centre pros and cons

+ The FODCA Trail is 100% singletrack
+ Tricky little climbs reward decent line choices
+ Descents vary from fast, to tighter and more technical
+ Lots of easy cycling in the area for families
+ Good, if short, DH tracks and jumps
− Short – but then there's the rest of the forest to explore
− Roots (if you can't ride them)

Directions

The FODCA Trail is just north of the crossroads between the B4226 and the B4234 in the Forest of Dean. At the crossroads, head north on the B4234 and turn left after a couple of hundred metres, into what appears to be Gloucestershire Highway's Cannop Depot – the car park is beside the depot.

Grid Ref: SO 608118   **Sat Nav:** GL16 7EH

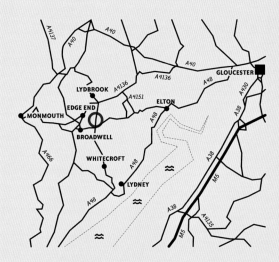

The trails

FODCA TRAIL	
DISTANCE: 5KM	**TIME:** 0.5–1HR
EFFORT: 2/5	**TECHNICALITY:** 3/5

The FODCA Trail is a short, but surprisingly tricky XC loop. Entirely singletrack, it follows dirt singletrack through the woods. Some sections are relatively smooth and fast, but much of the trail is covered in roots. As a result, line choice is critical, particularly on some of the short but tough climbs encountered along the route. The corners vary in style and difficulty, keeping you alert and on your toes, and the descents are all good fun, with the corkscrew section near the end being a particular highlight. A fine XC loop.

Other riding

The Forest of Dean contains mile upon mile of good singletrack, so go and explore. For families and those looking for an easier ride, there are plenty of wide, well-surfaced trails to choose between. If you're after the exact opposite, head straight up the hill, past the start of the FODCA Trail and you'll find a number of DH runs cut into the hillside. They are all short, but tricky to ride fast and feature some tight, steep corners and big jumps.

© MBR (MOUNTAIN BIKE RIDER) MAGAZINE

© MBR (MOUNTAIN BIKE RIDER) MAGAZINE

FRISTON FOREST

About the centre

Friston Forest isn't vastly dissimilar to many areas of woodland across the south east of England. However, lying on the south coast between Brighton and Eastbourne, Friston Forest sits at the foot of the South Downs – an area of the country blessed with a massive concentration of bridleways, and consequently, a fair few mountain bikers. Years ago, these riders used to hold XC races around Friston Forest. Now, although the races have gone and a waymarked trail has sprung up, you can see why it was used for XC racing. The riding isn't technical, but it is smooth, flowing and twisty. It's at its best in the summer as it can get very soggy in the wet. Perfect for riding fast.

Centre pros and cons

+ Woodland singletrack at its most flowing, root-dodging best
+ Maps available from car parks
− Signage could be better
− Can become very muddy

Directions

Seven Sisters: From Newhaven, follow the A259 through Seaford. The car park is signed on your left just over a mile after leaving the town.
Grid Ref: TV 520994   **Sat Nav:** BN25 4AD

Butchershole: No facilities, but you can pick up trail maps. To find it, continue along the A259 to Friston and take the road opposite the church, signposted Jevington. The car park is on your left after about a mile.
Grid Ref: TV 555994   **Sat Nav:** FRISTON

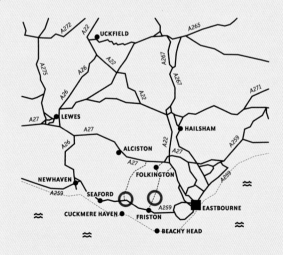

The trails

JEREMY COLE MOUNTAIN BIKE TRAIL

DISTANCE: 11KM	TIME: 1–2HRS
EFFORT: 2/5	TECHNICALITY: 2/5

This isn't so much a manmade route as a series of sections of woodland trail that have been walked/ridden/bashed into singletrack and then linked together. It's not surfaced and becomes pretty claggy in the wet, but visit when the ground is dry and the trails come alive. Although there's a fair amount of wide forest track on the route, there are enough long, twisty and fantastically flowing sections of singletrack that you forget about it instantly. There's nothing in the way of jumps or berms but, if you like fast XC singletrack, you'll be having too much fun to care.

Good to know

You can pick up the waymarked trail from either the Butchershole or Seven Sisters car parks. Maps are available at both, although all the facilities are at the latter.

SCOTT CRAMER

GISBURN

About the centre

Gisburn has always been a popular riding spot. Once hosting
XC and downhill races, it currently contains three easy XC loops
of varying lengths, a few entertaining downhill runs and some
hidden singletrack. However, there are big things planned for
the forest, with local bike shops and the Adrenaline Gateway
project (who were responsible for the trails in the nearby Lee
Quarry in Rossendale) getting involved to create waymarked
singletrack trails. This should ensure that Gisburn Forest
eventually contains something for everyone – short easy trails
for beginners; long, but straightforward trails for covering
distance; technical singletrack for 'trail' riders and downhill
trails for those looking for a little more excitement.

Centre pros and cons

+   Pleasant setting
+   Great for easier riding and for covering distance
+   Lots more planned for the future!
–   No waymarked technical XC riding (at present)

Directions

From Skipton, head north west towards Kendal on the A65 to
Long Preston. In Long Preston, turn left onto the B6478 towards
Clitheroe. Follow this through the villages of Wigglesworth and
Tosside and then turn right up a minor road signed to Gisburn
Forest. Park at Cocklet Hill car park, which is on your right
immediately after entering the forest.

Grid Ref: SD 745550   **Sat Nav:** SLAIDBURN

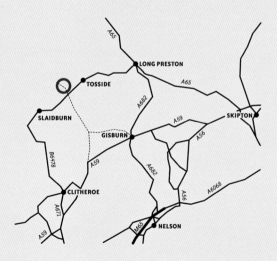

The Trails

PURPLE ROUTE	
DISTANCE: 9KM	**TIME:** 0.5–1HRS
EFFORT: 1/5	**TECHNICALITY:** 2/5

GREEN ROUTE	
DISTANCE: 12KM	**TIME:** 0.75–1.5HRS
EFFORT: 2/5	**TECHNICALITY:** 2/5

RED ROUTE	
DISTANCE: 16KM	**TIME:** 1–2HRS
EFFORT: 3/5	**TECHNICALITY:** 2/5

Gisburn's easy XC loops follow forest road and well-surfaced singletrack around the forest. Essentially, they are made up of one long route (the red) with two shortcuts, making the trail suitable for riders of varying levels of fitness. The routes are technically straightforward – mainly forest road with short sections of well-surfaced, but enjoyable (especially on the full red loop) singletrack – and so more suited to beginner and intermediate riders. They can be ridden in either direction, although we'd recommend riding them as anti-clockwise loops as this means that the more interesting riding is taken downhill on the return leg home.

Good to know

- There are a few downhill runs in Gisburn. The easiest way to find them is to follow the red route and keep an eye out – they're pretty obvious, starting from a clearing and dropping into the woods on the left.
- More modern development is planned at Gisburn – watch this space…

JOHN COEFIELD

GRIZEDALE

About the centre

Grizedale seems a strange location for a trail centre. The Lake District contains some of the best mountain biking in the UK – so why add a manmade trail? Of course, the same could be said of many other areas and, as with them, the centre has added a reliable, all-weather ride to the area. In fact, this trail is ideal for intermediate riders wanting an enjoyable, but not overly technical ride. That's not to say that the trail is easy – it's rocky in places and there's a fair bit of relatively narrow and off-camber north shore – but this just serves to make it a great place to improve your skills.

Centre pros and cons

+ Entertaining singletrack riding – not too hard, not too easy
+ It's in the Lake District
+ There are several easier waymarked routes through the forest
+ Good facilities
− More experienced riders will prefer the awesome natural riding found on the Lake District's extensive network of bridleways

Directions

Head south out of Hawkshead, turning right up a tiny lane signposted to Grizedale just as you leave the houses.
The centre is on your right after around 2 miles.
Grid Ref: SD 335943   **Sat Nav:** LA22 0QJ

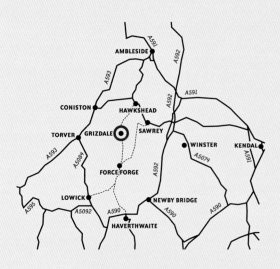

The trails

THE NORTH FACE TRAIL	
DISTANCE: 16KM	**TIME:** 1–2HRS
TECHNICALITY: 3/5	**EFFORT:** 3/5

The North Face Trail isn't overly technical. There are no jumps
or drops and there is a fair amount of fire road. There is,
however, a pleasant switchback climb, a few entertaining
sections of boardwalk and plenty of singletrack. The latter
varies from stony climbs to rocky traverses to fast, smooth
descents. It's good stuff, particularly the final swooping descent
to the visitor centre, rideable by relatively inexperienced riders
but still enjoyable for better riders going at higher speeds.
Add a great setting and you have decent ride, well-suited to
intermediate riders, that should keep you going for an hour or so.

Other riding

There are several other marked trails in Grizedale Forest.
The 3km **Goosey Foot Tarn Trail** begins from Moor Top car
park, back up the steep hill towards Hawkshead from the
visitor centre, and follows relatively flat, wide trails.
The **Grizedale Tarn Trail** is 9.5km long and begins from the
Bogle Crag Car Park, south of the visitor centre. The **Moor Top**,
Hawkshead Moor and **Silurian Way** trails are 11km, 16km and
22.5km respectively and all start from the visitor centre. Other
than that, get a map and use your imagination – you're in the
middle of the Lake District!

JOHN COEFIELD

JOHN COEFIELD

GUISBOROUGH

Centre pros and cons

+ The black presents technically able riders with an enjoyable, rooty challenge
+ There's a technically easy, but tiring trail to get you fit
− The waymarked riding is either easy or hard – there's nothing in between

Directions

Guisborough (the town) lies just west of Middlesborough on the A171, at the north west corner of the North York Moors. From Guisborough, head back towards Middlesborough on the A171, turning left (south) onto the A173 towards Stokesley at the first roundabout on the dual carriageway section of road. The car park is on your left after 200 metres.

Grid Ref: NZ 585152   **Sat Nav:** TS14 8HD

About the centre

Guisborough Forest is a fairly small set of woods at the north west corner of the North York Moors. Set on the side of a steep hill, there are two trails for mountain bikers. The first, graded blue, strikes out along forest roads and climbs steeply into the woods. It's technically easy and a good ride for the fit, but technically shaky. The black, meanwhile, is certainly not a trail for beginners, climbing incredibly steeply to the top of the hill before tackling some pretty technical and rooty trails. There's no waymarked trail here for intermediate riders, although there are plenty of non-marked trails to explore.

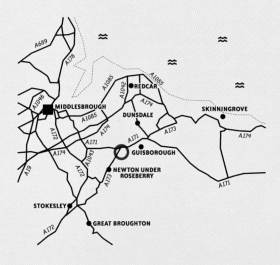

The trails

BLUE	
DISTANCE: 7KM	**TIME:** 0.5–1HR
EFFORT: 2/5	**TECHNICALITY:** 1/5

Graded blue for effort, rather than for technical difficulty, this route sticks to forest roads and easy tracks, but packs in a lot of climbing over its seven kilometres. It shares its initial climb through the woods with the black route, heading out along level terrain for a short distance before turning uphill. The climbing has some steep sections (perfectly rideable) and is never difficult – it's just long! Eventually turning downhill, the trail takes some straight, slightly narrower dirt trails to drop fast out of the woods into fields. A quick traverse of these sees you back into the woods with a short ride to the car park.

BLACK	
DISTANCE: 12KM	**TIME:** 1–2HRS
EFFORT: 4/5	**TECHNICALITY:** 4/5

Exploring some of the more interesting trails in the forest, and giving you a tempting glimpse of unmarked sections of singletrack, the black is a technically challenging trail. There's also no hiding from the massive climb to the top of the route – which, although all on easy trails, gets comically steep in places. Once you've got to the top and had a breather, the trail ducks onto singletrack through the woods. There are some tight corners, a few steep descents and some wide sections with multiple line choices. It's all good fun, but it's the roots splattered across the trails that make them technically challenging – if you can't ride them, you'll be going nowhere fast.

DAVID JOHNSON

HALDON

Centre pros and cons

+ Brilliant singletrack blue trail and gentle forest road green for the less experienced
+ Good, technical, red-graded singletrack
+ Reasonably extensive freeride area
− The XC trails could be a little longer

Directions

From Exeter, head south on the A38 towards Plymouth. Continue on the A38 towards Exeter racecourse and then follow brown tourist signs towards Haldon Belvedere off the main road. The car park is on your left, in the forest.

Grid Ref: SX 885847   **Sat Nav:** EX6 7XR

About the centre

Sitting just south of Exeter, Haldon Forest is the most southerly trail centre in the UK. At 3500 acres, it covers a large area, comprised mainly of pine woodland and areas of open heathland. It's full of wildlife: there's a managed butterfly area, a bird of prey viewpoint and it's not unlikely that you'll spot an adder or grass snake sunning itself on the trail at certain times of the year. Now, thanks to a grant from Sport England, several mountain bike trails have been added to the forest. For families, there are the Family and Adventure Cycle Trails, while experienced riders can chose between the tricky Red Route, the Freeride Area and the many singletrack trails dotted around the forest.

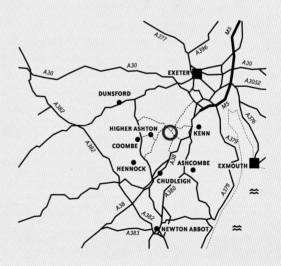

The trails

FAMILY CYCLE TRAIL	
DISTANCE: 5KM	**TIME:** 0.5–1HR
EFFORT: 1/5	**TECHNICALITY:** 1/5

Your typical family cycle trail. Haldon Forest's offering follows wide tracks around the forest. Generally well-surfaced, there are a couple of looser sections, but nothing too tricky. There are several surprisingly steep climbs on the route, although they aren't too long. An enjoyable and pleasant ride for families and those out for a gentle pootle.

ADVENTURE CYCLE TRAIL	
DISTANCE: 4KM	**TIME:** 0.5–1HR
EFFORT: 1/5	**TECHNICALITY:** 2/5

Cringeworthy name aside, the Adventure Cycle Trail is great fun. Running along solid, well-surfaced singletrack, it begins by zig-zagging across open ground before nipping into the woods and continuing to twist and turn its way back to the start. At speed, it flicks from corner to corner with a flow rarely found on such routes. Taken at a more leisurely pace… well, that's hard to do as it's so much fun to ride fast! Being so short and fairly flat, it's a route that beginners can enjoy, but it's also worth darting along, if you're here to ride the Red Route or Freeride Area.

Trails continue…

FORESTRY COMMISSION PICTURE LIBRARY / ISOBEL CAMERON

HALDON
continued...

RED ROUTE

DISTANCE: 11KM	TIME: 1–2HRS
EFFORT: 3/5	TECHNICALITY: 3/5

Much rougher than you'd expect, this is a rutted, rocky and rooty trail. It's also fast, making it surprisingly technical in places. There's a nice mix of singletrack. The trail begins by cutting along coarse ground, tackles a tough, stony climb and bounces over roots and holes in the woods before flying down a smooth, bermed descent. This is a good trail, even though it feels a little short. It passes the freeride area and offers glimpses of other sections of singletrack hidden in the woods.

FREERIDE AREA

DISTANCE: N/A	TIME: N/A
EFFORT: 2/5	TECHNICALITY: 4/5

Built by the Haldon Freeride guys, the freeride area is pretty extensive, with a lot of potential and a lot more planned for the future. Set near a couple of the better descents on the red XC route, there are a couple of parts to the freeride area (see the Haldon Freeride website). There are sections of north shore, a set of dirt jumps and some big kickers sending you out over some long gaps. The north shore has a corkscrew, some skinny sections and a few drops.

PAUL GROOM

HAMSTERLEY

About the centre

There's a lot of riding at Hamsterley. For XC riders, there's an easy beginner's trail, two long, mainly forest road routes and a technical singletrack outing that mixes manmade and natural trail features. You can also pick up a card from the visitor centre if you fancy testing your navigation and trying to find the trailquest controls dotted around the forest. If you'd rather test your skills, head for the downhill and 4X courses high above the visitor centre. Again mixing natural and manmade features, they're well worth a visit and often host races.

Centre pros and cons

+ Good for long, easy forest road rides
+ Entertaining and technical black route
+ Great for downhill and 4X riding
+ 'The Loop' is a great little skills area
- Not much 'flowing' singletrack for intermediate riders – although more is planned

Directions

From Durham, head south on the A690, towards Crook. Stay on this road, as it becomes the A689 at Crook, until you reach the roundabout junction with the A68. Turn left onto this, heading for Darlington and turn right after 3 miles, following signs for Hamsterley. Once in Hamsterley, turn right into the centre. After about a mile, cross the river and turn left onto the forest drive.

Grid Ref: NZ 092312   **Sat Nav:** DL13 3NL

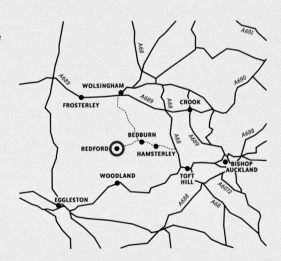

The trails

As the Visitor Centre sits at the bottom of a steep-sided valley, you've got two choices for riding. You could head off along the flat valley bottom, where it's relatively flat, or you could tackle the valley sides. The waymarked green route does the latter. It has, for a green-graded route, a fair amount of climbing with some surprisingly steep sections. Luckily, the trail sticks to easy tracks and forest or tarmac roads, and, as is usual in these circumstances, what goes up must come down. The descents are steeper than you might expect, but good fun. For a green route, this is a (worthwhile) challenge. There's always the forest drive if you want to dodge the climb, although you'll be dodging cars as well.

Although there's some singletrack at the beginning of the trail, this is a route for those who like to cover distance. After the initial narrow section of trail, which is well surfaced, easy and a fun way to start a ride, the route heads up the valley along the tarmac Forest Road. Turning off this, wide stony tracks climb away from the valley floor before a long, fast descent on similar tracks speeds back down again. Pleasant riding along the Forest Road returns to the visitor centre.

Trails continue...

© MBR (MOUNTAIN BIKE RIDER) MAGAZINE

© MBR (MOUNTAIN BIKE RIDER) MAGAZINE

HAMSTERLEY
continued...

RED	
DISTANCE: 22KM	TIME: 2–3HRS
EFFORT: 3/5	TECHNICALITY: 2/5

Extending the blue route by some considerable distance – and adding a fair bit of climbing – you'll certainly get fit riding the red. Essentially a longer and harder version of the blue, the two routes share the same start and the same, mainly forest road, style of riding. However, this trail adds bigger and steeper climbs, a slightly more varied surface and a lot more exposure to the elements. Tackle it on a windy day and you'll know about it! There are some technical sections of climbing, some rocky stretches and some narrower, rooty trails, but the trail sticks predominantly to easy fire roads. The descent is a long, fast forest road affair – great fun for riding a racing line at speed.

BLACK	
DISTANCE: 11KM	TIME: 1–1.5HRS
EFFORT: 3/5	TECHNICALITY: 4/5

Offering a completely different style of riding to the other XC rides at Hamsterley, the black is the route to pick for a technical blast. You'll still need to be reasonably fit – it may be short, but it's still hard work. There are some steep climbs, virtually no flat sections and you can expect to encounter a mix of natural and manmade trails. The latter throws rooty singletrack, steep and tricky climbing and some fast, off-camber descents into your path, while the manmade stuff offers twisting singletrack and fast berms. Currently the only technical XC trail here, it gets a little muddy in the winter, and never takes long to ride, but it is good fun and worth a visit.

DOWNHILL / 4X AREA	
DISTANCE: N/A	TIME: N/A
EFFORT: N/A	TECHNICALITY: 5/5

Well-known and respected, Hamsterley's downhill trails are tough tracks. Natural, rocky in places and very rooty, they're pretty technical. Add some jumps, drops and berms and you have courses that mix up manmade and natural features to great effect. The 4X course is relatively long and wide, with a good, sandy surface. You need to sign on at the shed if you want to ride the downhill or 4X trails. The downhill area has its own car park – follow the main directions, but carry straight on through Hamsterley village. The car park is on your right after about 3 miles (**Grid Ref: NZ 066288**).

Good to know

Hamsterley has a decent skills trail named 'The Loop'. A few hundred metres long, it's a good length and has various lines of differing technicality. There's some north shore, a few jumps and some fast corners – perfect for improving your riding.

DOUG INGLIS

HOPTON WOOD

AT A GLANCE
BEGINNERS: 2/3   **INTERMEDIATE:** 1/3   **ADVANCED:** 2/3

FACILITIES
(P) (↑)

THE TRAILS
Green	Green	N/A
Blue	Blue	1km
Amber	Blue	N/A
Red	Red	N/A
Black	Orange	N/A

NEAREST BIKE SHOP
Pearce Cycles, Ludlow (on site) – t: 01584 879 288

MORE INFORMATION
w: www.forestry.gov.uk
Shropshire Hills Discovery Centre, Craven Arms –
t: 01588 676 000

About the centre
Set on the side of a steep hill, Hopton Wood doesn't have any complete waymarked routes. Instead, it uses the ski-resort-like system of grading different sections of trail and then leaving you to create your own route. This is best done by picking up a map from the nearby Shropshire Hills Discovery Centre at Craven Arms. Most of the trails here are forest roads of varying steepness and there are only a couple of sections on singletrack. There are, however, a few rutted and rooty downhill runs that are a decent length and fairly technical. As a result, Hopton is pretty good for long, easy rides and for downhillers, but has little to offer other riders.

Centre pros and cons
+ Plenty of scope for long, hilly but technically easy riding
+ Good singletrack on the short blue route
+ The downhill courses are rough, rooty and relatively long
– Lots of fire road
– Grading of trails seems haphazard at best
– You'll need to pick up a map from the Shropshire Hills Discovery Centre – which is a short distance away

Directions
From Hereford, take the A49 north for 30 miles to Craven Arms. The Discovery Centre is on your right as you enter the village, if you need a map. If not, turn left in Craven Arms onto the B4368 (Clun Road) and then fork left onto the B4367. Turn right in Clungunford, towards Hoptonheath and then carry straight on past the station onto a minor road leading to Hopton Castle. Just under a mile after passing the castle ruins, turn left up a narrow track. The car park is a fair way up this track.

Grid Ref: SO 348778   **Sat Nav:** HOPTON CASTLE
Shropshire Hills Discovery Centre:
Grid Ref: SO 435824   **Sat Nav:** SY7 9RS

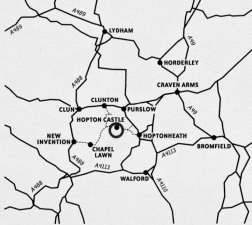

The trails

BLUE FAMILY ROUTE

DISTANCE: 1KM	TIME: 0.25–0.5HR
EFFORT: 1/5	TECHNICALITY: 2/5

This is a one-kilometre singletrack loop by the car park. Set on a gentle gradient, there's enough of a slope to have fun on the short descent, but not so much that the climb is a chore. The terrain is varied, ranging from tarmac-like to muddy and rooty and it's surprisingly technical in places for a 'family route'. A short, but entertaining route – a shame it's not longer.

FORESTRY COMMISSION PICTURE LIBRARY

GREEN/AMBER/RED

DISTANCE: N/A	TIME: N/A
EFFORT: N/A	TECHNICALITY: N/A

In a nutshell, green sections of trail tend to be fairly flat, amber stretches are a little steeper and reds are up again. The majority of the trails, regardless of colour, tend to be forest roads, or wide tracks. Green and amber trails are generally on very good, all-weather surfaces, whereas the red sections can be a little muddier. There are a couple of red-graded singletrack stretches of trail, the longest of which starts from the car park. They are natural trails running over dirt and roots, and are generally fairly steep and swoopy in nature. Pick up a map and explore.

BLACK

DISTANCE: N/A	TIME: N/A
EFFORT: 2/5	TECHNICALITY: 5/5

If you see a black-graded trail in Hopton, you'll be looking at a downhill track – so don't ride up it! There are a few different tracks to choose from, all of which are good. They are fairly worn and have, as a result, become fairly technical, mixing roots and deep ruts to create courses where working out the best lines will take a couple of runs. There are a few jumps and drops, but no mega steep or rocky sections. Worth a visit if downhilling is your thing.

Good to know

Pearce Cycles offers uplift weekends (booking essential). Call **01584 879 288** or visit **www.pearcecycles.co.uk**.

KIELDER

AT A GLANCE
BEGINNERS: 1/3 **INTERMEDIATE:** 3/3 **ADVANCED:** 2/3

FACILITIES

THE TRAILS
Deadwater . . . . Red 15km
Up and Over . . . . Black 2km
. . . . (addition to red)
Skills Area . . . . Various . . . . N/A

NEAREST BIKE SHOP
The Bike Place – t: 0845 634 1895

MORE INFORMATION
w: www.kieldertrailreavers.org.uk

About the centre
Sitting in the middle of a massive forest, the manmade trails at Kielder are a solid addition to the region. Built by the volunteer group Kielder Trail Reavers, the centre contains a red XC route with a short black-graded extension. The trails have plenty of singletrack, some tough climbing and run over some pretty sandy ground, meaning that the trails erode fast – increasing the difficulty of the already technical riding. There's not a massive amount of riding on offer (yet), but the centre's still a worthwhile destination for riders with a decent level of technical ability.

Centre pros and cons
+ Good black descent for confident riders
+ Solid red trail with some enjoyable singletrack climbs and descents
+ Good skills area
− Lots of forest road climbing
− Sandy trail surface wears fast

Directions
From Carlisle, follow the A7 north towards Hawick. After about 13 miles (just before Canonbie), turn right onto the B6357 and follow this through Newcastleton. Pick up signs for Kielder Water and Forest Park and in Saughtree turn right onto the C200 – a road which runs down to Kielder Water. Kielder Castle can be found about 7 miles down this road.

Grid Ref: NY 632936   **Sat Nav:** NE48 1HX

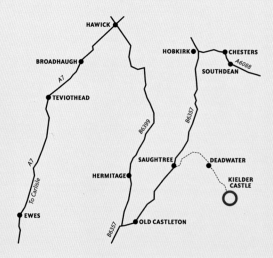

The trails

DEADWATER	
DISTANCE: 15KM	**TIME:** 1–2.5HRS
EFFORT: 3/5	**TECHNICALITY:** 3/5

An enjoyable route with some good sections of singletrack.
The trail begins with a couple of great descents through the
woods and around berms on a good trail surface. They're fast,
but you need to be controlled to ride them smoothly. After a
short section of forest road, the trail returns to singletrack, this
time through much darker woods on narrower trails. They're
rocky and rooty and have some technical sections, before the
route swings uphill for a good switchback climb. A long forest
road drag leads to the top of Deadwater and a wide, but fast
and rocky descent. Back onto singletrack, a technical climb
leads to the final descent, which swings around berms and
down into a flowing dirt section. Good fun.

UP AND OVER	
DISTANCE: 2KM (ADDITION TO RED)	**TIME:** 1–2.5HRS
EFFORT: 3/5	**TECHNICALITY:** 4/5

Kielder's black route branches off the red, missing out the final
descent of that trail and adding a tricky climb and technical
descent. After leaving the red, the trail climbs steeply uphill on
a loose surface. Difficult rock sections require good skills and
perseverance to clean, and some narrow (and low) north shore
checks your balance. The descent is steep and rough.
Alternating between fast jumps and berms and slower squeezes
between trees and stone staircases, it's a nicely varied trail. It's
a trail that rewards positive riding – especially over the gap
jump at the end. It's tiny, and confident riders will jump it
without a thought, but, whatever you do, don't try and roll it…

Good to know

- Campsite and youth hostel both within riding distance.
- More routes are planned at Kielder, including an easier,
  blue-graded route, which should be open by the end of 2008
  and which will increase the centre's suitability for less-
  confident riders.

MARK PINDER

MARK PINDER

QUEEN ELIZABETH COUNTRY PARK

About the centre

The Queen Elizabeth Country Park is in a great location. It's easily accessible by car, lying on the A3 just north of Portsmouth. It also sits on the South Downs Way, meaning that you can ride in from elsewhere, or use the park as the starting point for a longer ride. The Park itself is the largest in Hampshire, and popular with walkers and horse riders as well as cyclists, so you'll need to watch out for them. There are two volunteer-built waymarked routes – one on wide tracks, one on singletrack. Unfortunately, although the riding is good fun, neither route is particularly long and there's not quite enough to fill an entire day.

Centre pros and cons

+ The orange route contains some good singletrack and is a pleasant trail that a wide range of riders can enjoy
+ The purple ride makes a good circuit for fitter beginners and families (it may be a bit steep for young children though)
– Watch out for other users
– Short
– If you've never ridden on wet chalk, you'll be in for a slippery surprise

Directions

The Queen Elizabeth Country Park lies on the east side of the A3, about 3 miles north of the Portsmouth stretch of the A3(M). It's literally beside the A3 and is well signposted.

Grid Ref: SU 720182   **Sat Nav:** PO8 0QE

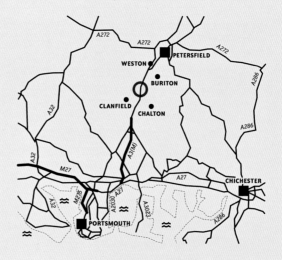

The trails

PURPLE ROUTE

DISTANCE: 6KM	TIME: 0.5–1HR
EFFORT: 2/5	TECHNICALITY: 2/5

Aimed at beginners, the purple route follows good, wide tracks through the forest. There's even a section of decent singletrack near the end – it's wide enough to be easily rideable, but runs downhill and weaves around a bit, ensuring that it's also fun. However, you'd better be reasonably fit if you fancy a crack at this route, as it's set on the side of a big hill and kicks off with a stiff climb. It's not a problem if you have to get off and walk as it's the only climb in the route and, after all, what goes up must come down.

ORANGE ROUTE

DISTANCE: 5KM	TIME: 0.5–1HR
EFFORT: 2/5	TECHNICALITY: 3/5

In a nutshell: a short singletrack loop in the woods. In slightly more detail, the route begins with a short, but steep climb before ducking into the trees for a descending traverse. A rooty climb regains lost height before a bermed descent on a chalky surface drops down to a fire road. Another steep climb leads to a much faster, rooty and off camber descent to the car park. You need to watch your lines over the roots and around the chalky corners, particularly in the wet, when a wheel out of place will have you on your back in the blink of an eye.

MARC DOBSON

ROSSENDALE
Lee Quarry

About the centre

The mountain bike trails in Lee Quarry, near Bacup in Lancashire, are part of the 'Adrenaline Gateway' project. This scheme aims to establish the Pennine area of Lancashire as a top-draw destination for those interested in the outdoors. For mountain bikers, this means the development of two areas: adding more XC routes to the beautiful Gisburn Forest, and building a cross-country loop and trials area in the industrial Lee Quarry. As we're concerned with the latter here, we'll tell you that there's one, fairly short trail at Lee Quarry (although it's well worth riding multiple laps), a trials area that's best-suited to committed trials riders and plenty to look at.

Centre pros and cons

+ Technically interesting and entertaining riding
+ The old quarry setting is a nice and pretty interesting change to the usual pine forest trails
+ Trials area for those who can hoppity-hop
– Short (do a few laps!)
– No facilities

Directions

From Manchester's M60 ring road, take the M66 north, following signs for Rawtenstall. When the motorway ends, continue onto the A56, and then take the A682, and A681, following signs to Bacup. Parking is on your right, in Futures Park, roughly 4 miles after joining the A681 and opposite the Post Office and the Royal Oak pub. To find the trails, head to the back right of Futures Park, pass the houses and climb the wide trail up to the obvious quarry.

Grid Ref: SD 866211   **Sat Nav:** OL13 0BB

The Trails

RED TRAIL

DISTANCE: 5KM	**TIME:** 0.25–0.75HRS
EFFORT: 2/5	**TECHNICALITY:** 3/5

BLACK EXTENSION

DISTANCE: 1KM	**TIME:** 10 MINS
EFFORT: 2/5	**TECHNICALITY:** 4/5

As you'd expect from a trail set in a disused quarry, the riding here is rocky and has plenty of edges you don't want to fall off... The first half of the trail is almost all climbing, and is almost all on wide, easy tracks and simple singletrack. It's not as bad as it sounds though, as there are plenty of things to look at and you pass the trials area on the way. It's the second half of the ride that makes the trail. The red descends on good, fast singletrack that flows nicely back down to the base of the quarry via some entertaining twists and turns. The black extension, meanwhile, throws in some rocky challenges, with stone spines, staircases and (avoidable) drops. It's a short trail, but well worth a visit.

JOHN COEFIELD

SHERWOOD PINES

Centre pros and cons
+ Loads of hidden woodland singletrack
+ New manmade trail on the way
+ Easy routes for families
+ Loads more planned
− No hills, so no climbs or descents

Directions
From Mansfield, pick up the A6030 heading north east, following signs for Clipstone and Ollerton. Follow the road out of town and throw Clipstone and Old Clipstone. Shortly after passing under the railway bridge, turn right into the well-signposted Sherwood Pines.

Grid Ref: SK 612637 **Sat Nav:** NG21 9JL

About the centre
If you're heading for Sherwood's singletrack, make sure you head for the Forestry Commission-controlled Sherwood Pines, and not Sherwood Forest's visitor centre. In the first, you can ride pretty much anywhere you like (obey the signs) whereas in the second, you're more limited in your riding and will have to dodge small children being taken to see where Robin Hood used to live. Sherwood Pines has always been popular with riders coming to hunt out the fast woodland singletrack that litters the area. It's also criss-crossed by wide forest tracks that make pleasant rides for those wanting an easier ride. There's also now the purpose-built and waymarked singletrack Kitchener trail – perfect for first time visitors looking for a fun ride without getting lost!

The Trails

SINGLETRACK	
LENGTH: N/A	**TIME:** N/A

FOREST ROADS	
LENGTH: VARIOUS	**TIME:** N/A

KITCHENER TRAIL	
DISTANCE: 10KM	**TIME:** 1–1.5HRS
EFFORT: 2/5	**TECHNICALITY:** 2/5

Sherwood Pines is a great place to mountain bike. If you want easy trails, hit the forest roads, either on the waymarked routes or on your own. For singletrack, pick up the Kitchener trail – ducking and weaving through the trees, it's easy to ride but up there with the best when taken at speed. If you enjoyed that and are feeling adventurous, head away from the signposts onto some of the forest's more hidden singletrack – heading south west towards the railway lines from the visitor centre would be a good place to start. You'll find some very tight trails, some fast, open riding and a few jumps and drops to play on. All great fun. Throw in a few sets of dirt jumps and some ambitious plans for the future and things look even better!

Good to know

There's a lot planned in Sherwood, with more easy riding (green, blue and 'adventure trail' routes), jump and skills areas on the cards, so keep an eye out!

WIG WORLAND

STAINBURN

About the centre

Stainburn's black route is the most technical manmade XC trail in the UK. Fact. Built mainly by trail-builders extraordinaire SingletrAction, Stainburn is unlike any other trail centre. You don't come here to cover distance, to flow through corners or to admire the views. You come because it's hard, and you come to 'session' sections until you ride them clean. Yes, there is an 'easy' red route, but it's a fifteen-minute fast and furious affair – so that's not much if you can't ride black routes. There is an 'XC' route in the woods across the road, but it's made up of off-camber roots, rocks and drops – hardly easy!

Centre pros and cons

+ Great for technically challenging riding
+ The black route features a very tough descent and a tricky climb – is this the most technically difficult manmade XC route in the UK?
+ The climbs are (nearly) as much fun as the descents – although you can miss them out if you want
+ The yellow route over the road contains some great technical riding of a more natural nature
+ Not a single piece of dull or uninspiring singletrack here
– The routes are on the short side (although the nature of the riding encourages you to repeat both individual sections and entire trails)
– The yellow route can become very muddy

Directions

From Harrogate, take the A59 west towards Blubberhouses. After 7 miles, turn left onto the B6451, signposted Otley. The car park is on your right after about 3 miles.

Grid Ref: SE 210509   **Sat Nav:** OTLEY

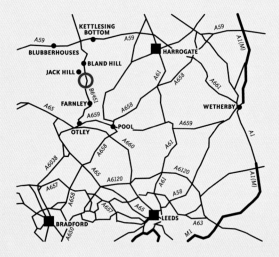

The trails

RED TRAIL	
DISTANCE: c.1KM	**TIME:** 0.25–0.5HR
EFFORT: 1/5	**TECHNICALITY:** 3/5

By far Stainburn's shortest and easiest route, the red is still a lot of fun. Swoop down from the car park, dodging rocks and roots and clambering over the odd rock obstacle (you can go around them, but if you need to do that, Stainburn probably isn't the place for you) before climbing through a short rock garden and into the woods. A few nice switchbacks later and you'll be diving down around low berms and hitting a couple of small jumps on your way back to the car park. Short and sweet.

DESCENT LINE	
DISTANCE: c.1KM	**TIME:** 5 MINS
EFFORT: 1/5	**TECHNICALITY:** 3/5

Turning off at the top of the red route, the Descent Line snakes through the woods around tight corners, and, picking up speed, heads out into the open. A few fast berms and some high-speed rock-sections lead to two sizeable drops that you can launch (if you dare), roll (if they're still growing) or avoid completely (if you're a chicken). Bigger, rougher berms and higher speeds lead to a steep climb back to the car park.

Trails continue...

DAVE WILSON

STAINBURN
continued...

NORWOOD EDGE

DISTANCE: 3.2KM	TIME: 0.5–1.5HRS
EFFORT: 3/5	TECHNICALITY: 4/5

Following the yellow-dot-trees, this might be a short XC route, but it's far from easy. Ducking and diving through the woods, the route is almost entirely natural singletrack. It's pretty technical and if your bike handling skills or fitness are lacking, it's going to show. The climbing is either steep or covered in roots. The descents are even steeper and rootier, and the flat bits, where you might expect a rest, are usually off-camber (and rooty). If you go in winter, you can throw a few peat bogs into the mix and take away most of the grip. Even so, for the determined and technically able, the route is a lot of fun.

BLACK TRAIL

DISTANCE: c.2KM	TIME: 0.5–1HR
EFFORT: 3/5	TECHNICALITY: 5/5

Think you're a good rider? Find slick slabs a doddle? Steep rock gardens easy? You can balance along boulder-spines and north shore no problem? And I take it you've got strong legs and well-rounded technical climbing ability? Good – because you'll need those skills and more to get around Stainburn's black. The descent is hard work and the climb is scary. It's a real technical challenge that rewards persistence, determination and a dogged refusal to move on until you've ridden a section clean. Everything is rideable but a dab-free lap would be a real achievement. Oh, and the chicken runs are just that.

PETE BYROM

SURREY HILLS

AT A GLANCE
BEGINNERS: 2/3   **INTERMEDIATE:** 3/3   **ADVANCED:** 3/3

FACILITIES

THE TRAILS
There are miles and miles of singletrack trails in the Surrey Hills.

NEAREST BIKE SHOP
Nirvana Cycles, Westcott – **t:** 01306 740 300
Head for the Hills, Dorking – **t:** 01306 885 007

MORE INFORMATION
w: www.hurtwoodcontrol.co.uk   **w:** www.redlandstrails.org

About the centre

The Surrey Hills consist of Leith, Holmbury and Pitch Hills – a large area of land managed by the Hurtwood Control just to the south west of London and open to mountain bikers. Not a trail centre by any stretch of the imagination, they contain mile upon mile of quality singletrack, including the waymarked Summer Lightning trail. The riding is woodland singletrack at its very best – fast, flowing and twisty, although it does get (understandably) busy and, in winter, muddy and eroded. There's also plenty of easier riding if singletrack isn't your thing. The Hurtwood Control asks that mountain bikers respect other users, don't create new trails and keep off sensitive areas.

Centre pros and cons

+ Some of the best woodland singletrack in the country
+ Mile upon mile of singletrack of a 'go anywhere nature'
+ Plenty of options for extended rides
+ Riding for all abilities
– You'll need a map, and even then, a willingness to explore and get lost is useful

Directions

These directions are for a car park at the base of Holmbury Hill – because it's between the other two hills and makes a good starting point for riding in the area. Pick up the A25 running between Guildford and Dorking and, about a mile east of Gomshall turn south onto the B2126, signposted to Holmbury St. Mary. After about a mile and a half, turn right up a minor road, signposted to the youth hostel.

Grid Ref: TQ 107447   **Sat Nav:** RH5 6NW

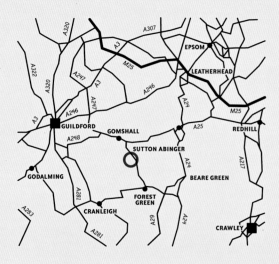

The trails

SINGLETRACK	
DISTANCE: N/A	**TIME:** N/A
EFFORT: 3/5	**TECHNICALITY:** 3/5

The main 'go anywhere' singletrack riding in the area is split over Leith Hill, which is the highest point in the south east, Holmbury Hill and Pitch Hill. All three are easily linked by decent bridleways. As a very rough generalisation, Pitch Hill tends to have the tightest, most technical trails and Leith Hill the most open and fastest with Holmbury Hill somewhere in the middle. The riding is, like all woodland riding in the south east, heavily affected by the weather (some tracks suffer terribly in the winter, so think about where you're riding) but dries into high-speed tree-dodging in good weather. There are several named trails in the area, all different and all good fun, including the waymarked Summer Lightning, a fast trail with berms, rough sections and roots. An absolutely brilliant area with some great riding.

Good to know

- Rides can be extended out into the surrounding countryside – head for Ranmoor Common for some testing climbs – and towards the train stations at Dorking and Box Hill if you're coming out of London.
- Maps – OS Explorers 145 and 146 will cover Pitch, Holmbury.

WIG WORLAND

SWINLEY FOREST

About the centre

You'll see more mountain bikers in Swinley Forest than walkers. They're drawn there by mile upon mile of superb singletrack. If you want sweeping trails, berms or tight corners through the trees, you'll find it in Swinley. If that's not your thing, there's a load of easier riding on the forest roads. Owned by the Crown Estate, the Forest is a private woodland where the local Gorrick and Berks on Bikes clubs have been let loose to build trails. In return, riders are required to buy a permit (£2 from The Look Out), which seems fair enough. You're unlikely to find every section of singletrack in the forest, but what you do find will keep you coming back for more.

Centre pros and cons

+ Absolutely brilliant singletrack
+ Virtually everybody should be able to find something they like here – you can cover distance on forest roads, hit the berms, jumps and drops near Surrey Hill or just follow the sweeping singletrack around for hours
+ The relatively straightforward, but twisty singletrack makes this a great venue for night riding

– You'll either need to follow a local or be prepared to visit the place a few times, expecting to get lost, if you want to find the best trails
– It can be very muddy after heavy rain but drains quickly
– Some trails are worn out through heavy use but are gradually being repaired

Directions

You can begin a ride in Swinley Forest virtually anywhere. If you've never visited before, The Look Out is a good place to start, as the visitor centre there sells permits, laminated maps and has a range of facilities. The Look Out is just off the A322, which runs between the M3 (Junction 3) and the M4 (Junction 4). Following brown tourist signs to The Look Out and Coral Reef, turn off the A322 onto Nine Mile Ride (the B3430) at a roundabout about 4 miles up from the M3. The Look Out is on your left after 100 metres.

Grid Ref: SU 876661   **Sat Nav:** RG12 7QW

The trails

SINGLETRACK	
DISTANCE: N/A	TIME: N/A
EFFORT: 2/5	TECHNICALITY: 3/5

It would be impressive if you were to ride in Swinley and NOT find any singletrack. It's everywhere! However, it's not marked or mapped and you'll have to be prepared to get lost on your first few visits to find anything – although it's well worth it. There are fairly flat, fast and sweeping trails over towards Crowthorne, big, bermed descents dropping down from Surrey Hill and long labyrinthine trails ducking through the trees elsewhere. While some of the predominantly dirt trails drain well in winter, others become heavily eroded and Gorrick MTB, who manage the trails, have been putting down a hard surface in places to help with this. An awesome venue for fast singletrack riding.

Good to know

- Day permits are available on the internet and from The Look Out in the forest, and can be purchased in advance. You can buy annual permits if you ride Swinley a lot.
- The Look Out car park shuts overnight. You can still drive out of the car park once its shut – just not in.

📷 ADAM TITLEY

THETFORD FOREST

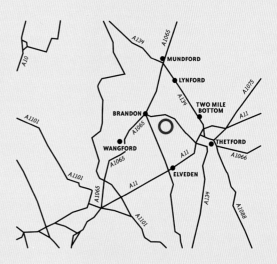
Centre pros and cons

+ The singletrack is fantastic – it's tight, twisting and there's loads of it
+ Anyone can enjoy the routes – twisty singletrack is always fun. If you disagree, ride faster...
+ There's riding here to suit most people
- There are no hills – so no descents and you can expect to do a lot of pedalling
- How much did you say it was to park!?

Directions
From Thetford, take Brandon Road (the B1107) north towards Brandon. The trails start at the High Lodge Forest Centre, which is signed on your left.

Grid Ref: TL 811851   **Sat Nav:** IP27 0AF

About the centre
Think of the Norfolk border and the flat expanses of eastern England and, let's be honest now, mountain biking isn't the first thing that springs to mind. Despite this, Thetford Forest contains some decent biking for riders of all abilities. For an easy day out on wide tracks, look at the green and blue routes on offer. If you'd rather ride singletrack, head for the red and black trails that twist and turn through the forest. Interestingly, many of these tight trails were created by motocross enduro events many years ago.

The trails

GREEN	
DISTANCE: 5/10KM	**TIME:** 1–2HRS
EFFORT: 1/5	**TECHNICALITY:** 1/5

For an easy couple of hours' riding, or a chance to spot some wildlife from the bike, the green route is a good choice. A 10km (or 5km if you take the shortcut) two-way trail along wide forest roads, the going is generally good, although there are a couple of puddles and a bit of mud at the back end of the route by the car park. Pleasant surroundings, ponds and woods full of birdlife make this a great trail to tackle with kids or just when you want a bit of gentle exercise.

BLUE	
DISTANCE: 13KM	**TIME:** 1–1.5HRS
EFFORT: 2/5	**TECHNICALITY:** 1/5

The main blue route is situated in the nearby Brandon Country Park, although it is easily linked to High Lodge to give a longer ride. Using, for the most part, wide and well-surfaced trails, the route does occasionally use narrower or looser tracks than the green route. Still, there aren't too many hills and it's never technical, so this is a good choice for those with slightly older children. Another pleasant ride.

Trails continue...

© MBR (MOUNTAIN BIKE RIDER) MAGAZINE

THETFORD FOREST
continued...

RED	
DISTANCE: 8/18KM	**TIME:** 1.5HRS
EFFORT: 3/5	**TECHNICALITY:** 2/5

BLACK	
DISTANCE: 17KM	**TIME:** 1–2HRS
EFFORT: 3/5	**TECHNICALITY:** 3/5

Despite weaving a tangled path through one of the flattest forests in the country, Thetford's Red route is a great laugh and surprisingly tiring. Nipping along tight tracks, dodging trees and flicking around corners, the trail follows dirt singletrack that encourages you to ride faster and faster until you realise you've sprinted the entire loop and are dribbling on your handlebars. The route traces a figure of eight loop and, to be honest, the first couple of kilometres are fairly uninspiring and you might find yourself tempted to take a short cut and miss out the second loop. Don't – the best is definitely still to come!

There's something about Thetford's singletrack that encourages even mild-mannered riders to charge along it like lunatics. Unfortunately, the sheer volume of the stuff on Thetford's black route means that, unless you're very fit, you'll have to exercise some restraint. And that isn't easy. The trail's snaking corners lure you into riding faster and faster. The quicker you go, the more you need to lean through the turns, the quicker you have to snap the bike back in line for the next and the better it feels. Addictive though it is, hold back a little as it saves the best for last.

Good to know

- At time of going to print, it'll cost you £6 to get onto the Forest Drive leading to the High Lodge visitor centre and the start of the trails – and they close the gates at night.
- Route maps are available for sale from the visitor centre or can be downloaded from the Forestry Commission website for free.

© MBR (MOUNTAIN BIKE RIDER) MAGAZINE

TIMBERLAND TRAIL

About the centre

The Timberland Trail is ten-minutes' ride from Bristol city centre. Built and maintained by local riders, it's a fun trail, especially considering its location. Set within Ashton Court Estate – which as you'd expect from a city park, is popular with many users – the trails can get busy. The riding's not technical, and is suitable for a wide range of riders, but, whatever you do, don't miss the section across the road in Abbots Leigh (see opposite for directions) as it contains the route's best singletrack. There's some really good riding to be had here, although, unfortunately, it's only short and you've got to brave Bristol's traffic to reach it – probably not worth travelling a great distance for.

Centre pros and cons

+ Fast, flowing riding
+ Good for beginners and more than enough fun for better riders
+ Considering the location, you could be forgiven for thinking you were a little further out of town
− The trail gets very muddy in the winter
− Muddy winters and lots of riders mean that there's not going to be a lot left to ride soon
− Watch out for other users

Directions

Ashton Court is 2 miles from Bristol city centre, on the south (non-city centre) side of the river. The trails begin just behind the gatehouse to the estate (there is parking available further in), which is on the A369 Abbots Leigh Road, that runs out towards Portishead, near the Clifton Suspension Toll Bridge. Come off the bridge, go straight ahead at the crossroads, and you're there.

Grid Ref: ST 558727   **Sat Nav:** BS41 9JN

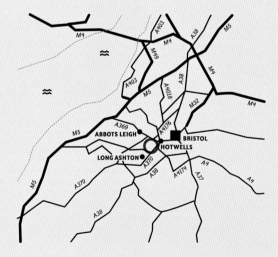

The trails

TIMBERLAND TRAIL

DISTANCE: c.9KM	**TIME:** 1–1.5HRS
EFFORT: 2/5	**TECHNICALITY:** 2/5

The trail officially runs anti-clockwise, although it's often ridden in the other direction, and with good reason. Try both and see which you prefer. In the summer, the trail dries hard and becomes a fast, tree-dodging speeder with plenty of corners to lean through and the odd rocky/rooty section to keep you alert. It's easy enough for beginners but plenty of fun to ride at speed. In the winter, however, the trail vanishes into the mud and becomes heavily eroded. The fast corners are replaced by slips and slides and you'd better watch out for the roots. Still fun to ride, you'll get plastered in filth and will accelerate trail wear dramatically.

Good to know

- The trail starts in a city park by a golf course. There are often children around and they probably won't appreciate you getting naked – come ready to ride.
- Don't miss the Abbots Leigh section of trail – follow the arrows out of Ashton Court through the high stone wall and turn left, then right down a lane. Keep going onto a bridleway and down the hill until you pick up the trail signs once more.
- If you want more, the nearby Leigh Woods offers fantastic woodland riding – full of corners and roots.

MIKE PRUETT

WHARNCLIFFE

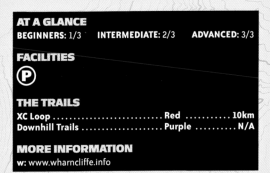

AT A GLANCE
BEGINNERS: 1/3   **INTERMEDIATE:** 2/3   **ADVANCED:** 3/3

FACILITIES
Ⓟ

THE TRAILS
XC Loop . . . . Red 10km
Downhill Trails . . . . Purple . . . . N/A

MORE INFORMATION
w: www.wharncliffe.info

About the centre

Wharncliffe is a steep, rocky and muddy wood on the northern edge of Sheffield with a big reputation. Best known for its downhill trails, with their super-technical rock gardens and drops, it is famed for being the training ground of three-times World Cup Downhill Champion, Steve Peat. In addition to the downhill runs, there are some good, technical sections of singletrack in the wood, which has played host to both downhill and XC races over the years. Unfortunately, Wharncliffe is also famed for the thick and gloopy mud which means the trails aren't a whole lot of fun to ride for much of the year…

Centre pros and cons

+ Technical XC riding
+ Several excellent, rocky and technical downhill runs
− The XC route turns into a quagmire in winter
− No facilities
− Little for beginners

Directions

Wharncliffe Woods are on the north-west side of Sheffield. From the city centre, follow the ring road up to the university and then drop down the hill on the dual carriageway onto Penistone Road (the A61), following signs to Barnsley. Stay on the A61 for about 5 miles, passing Sheffield Wednesday's Hillsborough ground and continuing into Grenoside. Turn left onto Norfolk Hill and climb to the crossroads with Main Street. Turn right and follow the road up into the woods. Park in the first main car park on your left.

Grid Ref: SK 325950   **Sat Nav:** GRENOSIDE

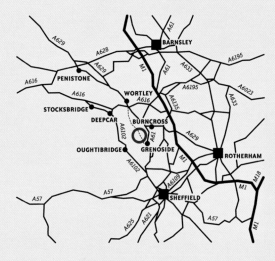

The trails

XC LOOP	
DISTANCE: 10KM	**TIME:** 1HR
EFFORT: 4/5	**TECHNICALITY:** 4/5

DOWNHILL TRAILS	
DISTANCE: N/A	**TIME:** N/A
EFFORT: N/A	**TECHNICALITY:** 5/5

Wharncliffe's old black XC loop was a technical trail that struggled up and down the steep hillside. It was also buried under thick mud for half the year. Now there's a new trail being built by local riders with help from SingletrAction. There are technical rock gardens, tricky corners and the hill is as steep as ever. It's fast in places, slow and 'thrutchy' in others – all good fun – and promises to develop into an awesome trail. Unfortunately, it's still a gloopy mess in winter so if you're visiting then, take your sense of humour with you.

Wharncliffe is best known for its downhill runs – of which there are several. They are highly technical – almost all feature massive gritstone rock gardens and drops. Some dive steeply down the hill, others contour and lose height more gradually. Some are natural, others are littered with jumps and berms. Currently, the local trail builders, the Wharncliffe Riders' Collective, are working with the Forestry Commission to designate part of the woods a 'Challenge Area', within which trail-building will be official. See their website (*www.wharncliffe.info*) for more details and please don't build outside this area.

◎ WIG WORLAND

WHINLATTER FOREST

AT A GLANCE
BEGINNERS: 1/3   **INTERMEDIATE:** 3/3   **ADVANCED:** 2/3

FACILITIES

THE TRAILS
Altura Trail . . . . Red 16km

NEAREST BIKE SHOP
Cyclewise (on site) – **t:** 01768 778 711
Keswick Mountain Bikes, Keswick – **t:** 01768 780 586

MORE INFORMATION
w: www.forestry.gov.uk

Centre pros and cons
+ Solid singletrack trail
+ Great location
+ Lots more planned!

Directions
From Keswick, take the A66 west towards Cockermouth.
After a couple of miles, enter the village of Braithwaite and
immediately turn left onto the B5292. Follow the road through
the village and up into Whinlatter Forest. The car park and
visitor centre will be on your right.

Grid Ref: NY 209245   **Sat Nav:** CA12 5TW

About the centre
Lying to the west of Keswick in the northern Lake District,
Whinlatter Forest is a great spot. An attractive, steeply-sided
forest, it boasts some great views out over Bassenthwaite Lake
and the surrounding area. It also contains the Altura Trail,
a figure of eight loop built by *Clixbys trailbuilders* and running
to the north and south of the main visitor centre.

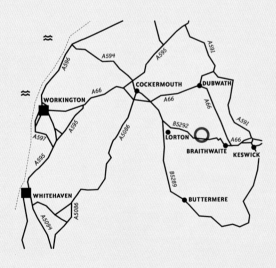

The Trails

ALTURA TRAIL

DISTANCE: 16KM	**TIME:** 1–2HRS
EFFORT: 3/5	**TECHNICALITY:** 3/5

Taken steadily, the relatively straightforward Altura Trail makes a pleasant ride. The woodland is pretty, the birds are probably singing and there are some great views to admire from the climbs. Hit with a bit more speed, the trail takes on a completely different character. Try not to touch the brakes through the flowing corners, big berms and jumps and you can add a massive dose of fun to the experience. Although relatively straightforward, this trail isn't a pushover – the climbs have some tight corners and there are a few sharp climbs, rocks and roots that might catch out the unwary. A great trail – fun for relatively inexperienced riders and fast riders alike.

JOHN COEFIELD

JOHN COEFIELD

TOP 10:
To Start Out On

Roughly in order of difficulty, here's the cream of the beginner-friendly crop:

1   Thetford
Easy, easy green and blue routes, and the harder routes aren't too tricky if you want to push yourself a little.

2   Glentrool
Two contrasting green routes and a singletrack blue extension if you're feeling good.

3   Haldon's blue and green
If only they weren't so short! A good green and a fantastic singletrack blue.

4   Drumlanrig
Trails you could ride with stabilisers right through to technical XC – Drumlanrig's all about improving.

5   Abriachan
A twisting green and a pleasant blue trail, sat high above Loch Ness.

6   Ae's Ae Valley
Smooth, flat singletrack. Perfect for the kids.

7   Glentress green
Easy, short singletrack, a beginner-friendly skills area and a brilliant blue to progress to.

8   Brechfa's Derwen Trail
You could ride this with your Gran – and you'd both have a brilliant time.

9   Learnie's blue routes
Smooth and swoopy. These might well be the best blue routes in the UK.

10 Carron Valley
Not for complete beginners, but great fun for those with a little more experience.

SECTION
SCOTLAND

FORT WILLIAM WORLD CUP DOWNHILL JOHN COEFIELD

ABRIACHAN

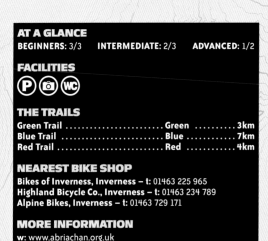
About the centre

Abriachan is an ideal centre for less experienced mountain bikers. Sitting high above Loch Ness, the trails were built after the members of the local community joined forces and purchased a large area of forest and open land, partly in order to develop and encourage recreational enjoyment of the outdoors. There are now three trails, each progressively more difficult than the last, and a dirt jump area – where, again, there are several lines of increasing difficulty. The green and blue trails give newer riders two well-surfaced routes to enjoy, whilst the red provides a more natural and technical difficult challenge for more advanced riders.

Centre pros and cons

+ Great green and blue-graded trails make this a good centre for beginners
+ The natural and technical red trail provides something for more advanced riders
+ The jump area has some good lines to learn on, but is interesting enough for confident riders
+ A good skills area by the green trail helps beginners to progress
− Basic facilities
− The trails are on the short side

Directions

Follow the A82 south from Inverness for 8 miles (13km) before turning north up a small, steep lane signed to Abriachan. In the village, fork left following signs to Abriachan Forest Walks. Turn left after the small loch.

Grid Ref: NH 540354   **Sat Nav:** ABRIACHAN

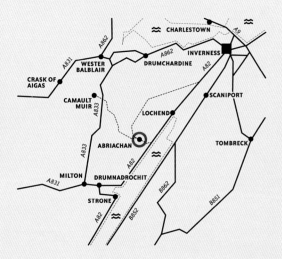

The trails

GREEN TRAIL

DISTANCE: 3KM	TIME: 0.5–1HR
EFFORT: 1/5	TECHNICALITY: 2/5

The green route makes a superb ride for beginners wanting to try 'proper' mountain biking. Following wide singletrack for its entire length, the trail is easy to ride, with a good, hard surface, a couple of gentle climbs and some fun descents. These descents pack in plenty of corners, some shallow berms and a few easy jumps (if you fancy them). Passing through picturesque surroundings, the route follows woodland streams and crosses open areas with expansive views. These add a lovely atmosphere to the ride, making this a trail that's about enjoying every aspect of riding.

BLUE TRAIL

DISTANCE: 7KM	TIME: 0.5–1.5HRS
EFFORT: 2/5	TECHNICALITY: 2/5

The blue route starts from a second car park further into the woods. You can reach it by car, or by a ten-minute ride from the green route. Another good trail for less-experienced riders, this is a narrower and longer version of the green route. The trail surface is still good and there are no technical obstacles, but the berms are a little higher and the climbs and descents longer. The trail takes you further away from your car and you'll get a real sense of what it means to be in the Scottish Highlands. Another enjoyable, yet relatively easy trail.

RED TRAIL

DISTANCE: 4KM	TIME: 1–2HRS
EFFORT: 3/5	TECHNICALITY: 4/5

The red route is very different to anything else at Abriachan. Branching off the blue, it follows technical, unsurfaced singletrack over rocks, roots and peat. Packing in lots of short but steep climbs and descents, it is a fairly tricky ride – especially in the wet when things get slippery. As with the blue route, the ride finishes in the jump area, which is surprisingly good. There are several lines, starting with some very small jumps and building up to some large table tops, with a few berms and more creative lines in between – good for learning on, reasonable for better jumpers.

Good to know

To reach the start of the blue and red trails by car, follow the forest road past the first car park and around to the left. You'll reach the second car park after a kilometre or so.

AE
7stanes

AT A GLANCE

BEGINNERS: 3/3   **INTERMEDIATES:** 3/3   **ADVANCED:** 3/3

FACILITIES

THE TRAILS

Ae Valley .... Green 9km
Ae Blue Route .... Blue 13.5km
Ae Line .... Red 24km
Ae Downhill .... Orange 1.6km

NEAREST BIKE SHOP

Ae Bike Shop and Café – w: www.ae7.co.uk
G and G Cycle Centre, Dumfries – t: 01387 259 483

MORE INFORMATION

w: www.ae7.co.uk   w: www.7stanes.gov.uk
w: www.upliftscotland.com

Centre pros and cons

+ Good for jumpy, bermy trails
+ A great green trail for beginners
+ There's the downhill course and the push-up-able Omega Man descent for downhillers

Directions

Follow the A701 north out of Dumfries towards Moffat. Turn left after 10 miles onto a minor road, signposted Forest of Ae. The centre is on your right, just after Ae village.

Grid Ref: NX 982901   **Sat Nav:** DG1 1QB

About the centre

Interesting fact: The village of Ae has the shortest place name in the UK. It's also been a popular downhill venue for several years, playing host to a number of races including the National Points Series. In 2005, the red-graded Ae Line was added to the area as part of the 7-Stanes development, with a green-graded route following shortly afterwards. The Ae Line is a bit of a departure from the norm, being an aggressive trail full of jumps and berms – so much so that its final descent, The Omega Man, has a push up track which is regularly used by downhill riders sessioning that section.

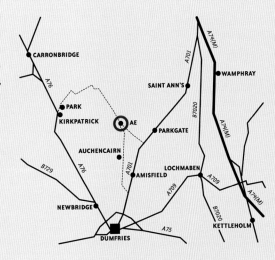

The trails

AE VALLEY

DISTANCE: 9KM	TIME: 1–1.5HRS
EFFORT: 2/5	TECHNICALITY: 1/5

AE BLUE ROUTE

DISTANCE: 13.5KM	TIME: 1.5–2.5HRS
EFFORT: 2/5	TECHNICALITY: 2/5

The Ae Valley Trail is a fantastic trail for inexperienced or young riders. Relatively flat with little climbing, it's roughly half forest track and half wide, smooth and easy singletrack. This means that not only is it a good way to go for an easy ride, it's also a fun introduction to real mountain biking as the wide singletrack twists and turns through the trees. Essentially, it's an easier version of a blue or red-graded trail – and that's always going to be more fun for beginners than ploughing along forest roads. There are a good few places to stop for a rest and a display of old ploughs to admire…

The recently-opened Blue Route follows the Ae Valley route for much of the way but extends this to take in more of the forest, with open forest road riding and sections of steady singletrack and boardwalk. Perfect if you're after a bit more than the Ae Valley, but don't feel up to the Ae Line.

The trails

AE LINE

DISTANCE: 24KM	TIME: 1.5–3HRS
EFFORT: 3/5	TECHNICALITY: 3/5

Cunningly named after the jump-filled A-Line trail in Whistler, the Ae Line is a fast, aggressive ride. However, at 24km it's definitely an XC trail and you can expect some climbing. A zig-zagging singletrack climb kicks off before pleasant trails lead to the typical Ae descents of The Face and The Edge. Both are great trails, diving around berms and over jumps but they're just warm ups for what's to come. Lower your saddle if you haven't already, as the final descent of The Omega Man descends fast over jumps and drops. Choose the red or black line (they're side by side so you can mix and match) – either way, it's so well built that even ground-loving riders will be grinning through the air and landing perfectly by the bottom – where they can push back up for another run.

AE DOWNHILL

DISTANCE: 1.6KM	TIME: 2.3 MINS (PRO), 5 MINS (NON-PRO)
EFFORT: N/A	TECHNICALITY: 5/5

The Ae Downhill course has played host to a number of races over the years and it's easy to see why. Starting at the top of Knocksepen Hill, the trail combines technical root and dirt sections with some massive manmade features. Expect rock gardens, muddy off-cambers and rooty bits, jumps, gaps and steep drops and you'd better be feeling good before launching into space over the big step down and around the enormous berms near the bottom of the course. If you're pushing up, follow the track opposite the Forestry Offices uphill and take the first major left. Otherwise, see ***www.upliftscotland.com*** for details of uplift days.

ARRAN

About the centre

Arran is a brilliant place for mountain biking. There's a wide array of fantastic, mainly natural trails, terrific views, and any ride on the island brings with it a real sense of occasion and adventure. Arran isn't a 'trail centre' as such – local riders have done a bit of trail building, mapped a few routes and dropped in a few waymarks – but you'll still need a map to get around. It does, however, have something for everyone. Roadies will appreciate the traffic-free environment, inexperienced mountain bikers can tackle the wider, less technical trails, while everyone else can hit the technical singletrack and steep climbs that litter the island. Definitely worth a visit.

Centre pros and cons

+ There's some awe-inspiring natural singletrack
+ There's some pretty good manmade stuff too…
+ Would you have considered visiting Arran otherwise?
+ Arran is an awesome place to visit. It's not known as 'Scotland in Miniature' for nothing
− Limited waymarking so take a good map

Directions

There are two ferry services to Arran – Ardrossan to Brodick and Claonaig to Lochranza. For most, the Ardrossan service is the more convenient; it's 30 miles from Glasgow, runs all year round and uses a reasonably large ferry. The Claonaig (on Kintyre) service is summer only and uses a smaller ferry, although it is a shorter crossing. You can take your car over, although bikes are cheaper. See **www.calmacbookings.co.uk** for details. The routes described here all begin in the town of Brodick.

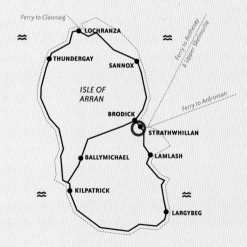

The trails

CASTLE BLUE

DISTANCE: 10KM	**TIME:** 0.5–1.5HRS
EFFORT: 2/5	**TECHNICALITY:** 1/5

By far the easiest of Arran's mapped routes, this relatively short route runs along good, wide trails in the grounds of Brodick Castle. The riding is straightforward, though hilly, and passes through some pleasant woodland. To find the route, you'll need to head north along the road out of Brodick (with your map) past the castle and turn onto a wide track. It's a good, enjoyable ride for the less-experienced, and there's plenty for children to look at, but it's probably not the one to pick if you've come to Arran to see the island.

BLUE

DISTANCE: 10KM	**TIME:** 1–2HRS
EFFORT: 2/5	**TECHNICALITY:** 2/5

The second of Arran's blue routes is a much better choice for exploring the island. Although short, it packs in a fair bit of climbing as good trails carry you up into the hills above Brodick, via a couple of picnic spots in great locations. Once up, some relatively technical singletrack drops and climbs over loose rocks. It's good fun, but a prickly penalty awaits if you veer off-line on the Gorse-lined trails. A fast and straight descent drops back into Brodick. A good introduction to Arran's 'proper' mountain biking.

Trails continue…

© MBR (MOUNTAIN BIKE RIDER) MAGAZINE

© MBR (MOUNTAIN BIKE RIDER) MAGAZINE

ARRAN
continued...

RED	
DISTANCE: 18KM	**TIME:** 1.5–3HRS
EFFORT: 3/5	**TECHNICALITY:** 3/5

Arran's red route loops south from Brodick towards the town of Lamlash, exploring the Clauchland Hills as it does so. There's a fair bit of climbing en route, but it's a small price to pay compared with the views and descents you get in return. Stiff climbing on the road and then on grassy tracks leads up to the route's 260m highpoint and an awesome stretch of natural singletrack, which is rocky, peaty and goes on and on and on. A good descent leads to the coast and the shops of Lamlash, before more climbing leads up to a final singletrack run back towards Brodick. Technical, hilly and lots of fun, this is a route most riders will appreciate.

BLACK	
DISTANCE: 35KM	**TIME:** 2.5–5HRS
EFFORT: 4/5	**TECHNICALITY:** 4/5

Arran's black is a big route, covering a lot of distance and tackling some stiff climbs. Beginning in Brodick, it joins the red and blue routes on the Clauchland Hills before dropping through Lamlash and climbing into the forest beyond. Wide trails carry you steadily south towards Whiting Bay, from where steep, loamy, manmade singletrack slices through thick pine forest. A stark contrast to the rest of the riding available on Arran, but still great fun. Trails shared with the routes described above then lead back to Brodick via some gentle climbing and gorse-lined singletrack. A tough route, both physically and technically, that covers a fair distance via a set of nicely varied trails.

Good to know

- The routes described here all begin in the town of Brodick.
- Rough maps of the routes described here can be found at **www.arranbikeclub.com** or picked up from the Tourist Information Centre on Brodick.

© MBR (MOUNTAIN BIKE RIDER) MAGAZINE

© MBR (MOUNTAIN BIKE RIDER) MAGAZINE

BALBLAIR

About the centre

Balblair is all about technical XC riding. Designed by Rik Alsop, it's a relatively out-of-the-way centre, where you are taken out into the hills on natural-feeling trails. Aimed well and truly at experienced riders, the fantastic black route features rock slabs, steep loose descents and the odd bit of boardwalk to keep the flow going nicely. In addition, you get great views and peaceful surroundings – all the makings of a great ride. The blue route, meanwhile, is relatively short, but has a cracking final descent and, if combined with a visit to the nearby Carbisdale trails, would make a good day out for beginner/intermediate riders.

Centre pros and cons

+ Fantastic, natural-feeling singletrack on the black trail
+ Good technical descents and climbs
+ Lovely area, great views and a nice 'feel' to the trail create a great atmosphere
+ Balblair is relatively unknown, which keeps the trails nice and quiet
− No facilities on site, but toilets, café and bike hire at Carbisdale Castle Youth Hostel

Directions

Take the A9 north from Inverness. After around 35 miles, turn left onto the A836, signed to Bonar Bridge. Follow this road through Bonar Bridge, and the trails begin from a car park on your left about 1.5 miles (2.5km) outside the town.

Grid Ref: NH 604930   **Sat Nav:** BONAR BRIDGE

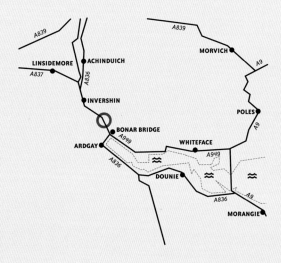

The trails

BLUE	
DISTANCE: 3KM	**TIME:** 0.5–1HR
EFFORT: 3/5	**TECHNICALITY:** 3/5

Balblair's blue route is short, but packs in a fair bit of climbing and descending on a mix of forest road and singletrack. The trail surface is fairly rough – more so than you might expect for a blue, but isn't too tricky to ride. Once the mainly forest road climb is done, you can relax in the knowledge that it's all downhill (in the right way) from then on. The trail soon narrows and picks up speed, before turning onto a long, flowing series of tight switchbacks and sharp corners that spit you out, grinning, into the car park.

BLACK	
DISTANCE: 7.5/11.5KM	**TIME:** 1.25–2.5HRS
EFFORT: 4/5	**TECHNICALITY:** 4/5

Natural feeling, technical and great fun, Balblair's black route begins with some fairly stiff climbing and traversing along what appear to be sheep tracks and over slabs of white rock. The rock sections, of which there are lots, are tricky in places. They're not hard enough to stop you, but fiddly enough to punish lapses in concentration. A bit of boardwalk gives you a breather before the trail fires off downhill around tight, rough berms – when the trail breaks away from its natural feel it does so well! More rough singletrack leads to an awesome descent, which drops you steeply around tight corners and rocky switchbacks for a quick blast along the amazing final stretch of the blue route.

Good to know

- If you want to combine a trip to Balblair with a visit to the Carbisdale trails, you can either drive round or ride up towards Invershin station and cross the footbridge alongside the railway track.
- The Balblair and Carbisdale trails often get listed together as the 'Kyle of Sutherland' trails.

FORESTRY COMMISSION PICTURE LIBRARY / JOHN McFARLANE

CARBISDALE

About the centre

Named after the attractive Carbisdale Castle (now a youth hostel) and starting right beside it, the trails here are short and best-suited to less experienced riders. That's not to say that the trails aren't enjoyable, but they are not technical and can both be ridden in well under two hours, even going at a steady pace. If you wish to make a day of it, riding the trails and then heading to the nearby Balblair (blue and black trails) would make for a decent amount of riding.

Centre pros and cons

+ A nice set of trails for intermediate riders (although limited for complete beginners and advanced riders)
+ Can be combined with the nearby Balblair blue to make a good day out
+ Handy for the youth hostel
− Short but more riding on offer at Balblair

Directions

Take the A9 north from Inverness. After around 35 miles, turn left onto the A836, signed to Bonar Bridge. Follow this road to the village of Culrain, and turn left just after the railway station, following signs for Carbisdale Castle Youth Hostel. Follow the signs into the youth hostel grounds – the trails begin from a small car park at the bottom of the drive.

Grid Ref: NH 574953   **Sat Nav:** IV24 3DP

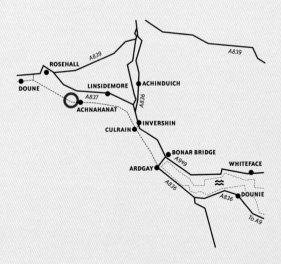

The trails

BLUE	
DISTANCE: 3KM	**TIME:** 0.5–1HR
EFFORT: 1/5	**TECHNICALITY:** 2/5

Running over a hard, stone-based surface, Carbisdale's blue route is almost entirely singletrack. Relatively wide, it's an entertaining trail with the odd rock to jump off and the odd slab of grippy rock to ride along. These are all avoidable, meaning that the trail can be enjoyed by riders with varying technical abilities. There are plenty of short descents, with Hissing Sid – a series of wide hairpins – being a particular highlight.
The turns, of which there are plenty, are generally all wide and easy, and, as with all good singletrack, the better you ride it, the better it gets.

RED	
DISTANCE: 4.5KM	**TIME:** 0.5–1HR
EFFORT: 2/5	**TECHNICALITY:** 2/5

This is one of the easier red-graded routes around, being on a par with some of the trickier blue routes, such as Kirroughtree's, so if you usually ride blue routes and worry about grades, you may as well give it a whirl. The route is an extension of the blue, but, as you would expect, it is a little harder. It follows narrower singletrack over a more varied surface, running along dirt trails as well as hardpacked stone. This extension adds two climbs and descents to the ride, with some tighter and trickier corners. There are no overly-technical sections. although as with the blue route, there are options to test you if you want to.

Good to know

- If you've ridden the trails and fancy some more riding, the nearby Balblair trails have blue and black-graded routes. You can either drive to them via Bonar Bridge, or follow the railway line down, turning right along the A836.
- The Balblair and Carbisdale trails often get listed together as the 'Kyle of Sutherland' trails.

📷 FORESTRY COMMISSION PICTURE LIBRARY / JOHN McFARLANE

CARRON VALLEY

Centre pros and cons

+ The different sections of singletrack all have their own, individual, character
+ Good signage and trail design make it easy to take shortcuts or ride sections again
+ The Runway is a great place for confident intermediate riders to get their wheels off the ground
+ More facilities and trails are planned
+ Easily accessed from several major cities
− The trail won't fill a day's riding unless you go around twice

About the centre

Carron Valley sits bang in between Edinburgh and Glasgow, putting it within easy reach of a large number of riders. A long-established mountain biking spot with some great trails, the addition in 2006 of the red route, has proved to be popular with riders. Apart from a couple of short sections, it's a straightforward route and is not too technical – making it a good choice for less able riders. However, pick up the speed, start leaning around the corners and hitting the jumps hard and you have a great trail for the more experienced. Clever route design and good signposting makes it easy to ride your favourite sections over again.

Directions

From Stirling, turn off the M80 at J9 onto the A872. Follow this south towards Denny, forking right and staying on the A872 as you enter the town. After half a mile, turn right onto the B818, following signs for Fintry. After 5 miles, go through Carron Bridge. The car park for the trails is on your left 1.5 miles (2.5km) further along the road.

Grid Ref: NS 722838   **Sat Nav:** FK6 5JL

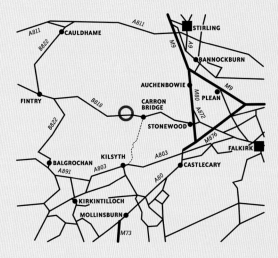

The trails

RED TRAIL

DISTANCE: 10.5KM	**TIME:** 1–2HRS
EFFORT: 3/5	**TECHNICALITY:** 3/5

Carron Valley's red trail is a great route consisting of four very different sections of singletrack. First up is Pipedream – a gentle singletrack climb with a couple of off-camber switchbacks and the odd downhill so you don't get bored. Height gained, next up is Eas Dubh, which takes you over the rocky 'Kelpies Staircase' and down around a series of wide switchbacks. Following this comes the Cannonball Run – a high-speed section of singletrack with gently-bermed corners. The last section, The Runway, is well named (it's actually named because it's under Glasgow Airport's flight path), as it's a fast run over jumps, encouraging you to pick up speed and take off. Great fun.

Good to know

The main car park is locked overnight, so don't get caught out!

HOWARD COTTON

HOWARD COTTON

COMRIE CROFT

AT A GLANCE
BEGINNERS: 1/3   **INTERMEDIATE:** 3/3   **ADVANCED:** 2/3

FACILITIES

THE TRAILS
Red .... Red 5.5km

NEAREST BIKE SHOP
Comrie Croft Bikes, on site – t: 01764 670 140

MORE INFORMATION
w: www.comriecroftbikes.co.uk

About the centre

A croft is defined as a small piece of farm land. Comrie Croft is a small piece of land with a difference – there's a friendly youth hostel in the middle and some great singletrack winding through the area immediately around it. The crofters who run the hostel are responsible for hand-crafting the trail, which has a very natural feel to it. Currently around five and a half kilometres long with a fair amount of singletrack, more trail building is planned. There's plenty of other good riding in the area – decent mountain biking and some easier stuff for families, so there's plenty to do, even if the trail only takes an hour or so.

Centre pros and cons

+ Enjoyable singletrack with a natural feel to it
+ Friendly and helpful people running the hostel and trails
+ Easily accessible from Edinburgh and Glasgow
+ Perthshire is a beautiful area of Scotland
− There's only about an hour's riding here

Directions

From Perth, take the A85 west towards Crieff. Staying on the A85, go through the town and Comrie Croft Youth Hostel is signed on your right after 4.5 miles (7.5km) – watch out as the signs don't give you much warning!

Grid Ref: NN 803230   **Sat Nav:** PH7 4JZ

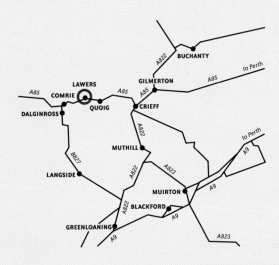

The trails

RED

DISTANCE: 5.5KM	**TIME:** 0.5–1HR
EFFORT: 2/5	**TECHNICALITY:** 3/5

The trail begins with a climb up a wide track, passing through a couple of fields of sheep before hitting the first stretch of singletrack climbing. Crossing open ground before ducking into the woods, the trail is dotted with rocks and roots. It's reasonably technical – not overly hard, but fiddly enough to require concentration. The trail continues, in the same tricky manner, up short climbs and down steep little descents – all good fun. Narrow dirt tracks lead into fields (watch out for the sheep) where it's easy to lose the trail, and onto the final descent. Smoother than the earlier singletrack, this is a flowing track through open woodland, rounding off an enjoyable, if short, ride.

JOHN COEFIELD

JOANNA DAXELL

DALBEATTIE
7stanes

AT A GLANCE
BEGINNERS: 2/3   **INTERMEDIATE:** 3/3   **ADVANCED:** 3/3

FACILITIES

THE TRAILS
Ironhash Trail .... Green 11.5km
Moyle Hill Trail .... Blue 14km
Hardrock Trail ...... Red (optional black sections) .. 27km

NEAREST BIKE SHOP
G and G Cycle Centre, Dumfries – t: 01387 259 483

MORE INFORMATION
w: www.7stanes.gov.uk

About the centre

Dalbeattie is a must-ride 7 Stanes trail centre. The fantastic granite-splattered singletrack, which typifies the centre, gives it its own, distinctive character. It has a good range of trails and, despite being flatter than the other 7 Stanes and so lacking somewhat in climbs and descents, still manages to fit in some excellent riding, including one of the most famous features at any trail centre: The Slab. This is a steep, 14-metre high lump of granite forming one of the red-graded, Hardrock Trail's descents. It's appeared in numerous photos yet often gains a couple of metres in height, several degrees in steepness and becomes endowed with wheel-sized drainage gullies once you're sat at the top. If you're not after technical riding, the green and blue trails offer straightforward, mainly forest road trails – perfect for an easy ride.

Centre pros and cons

+ The Slab – one of the most famous trail features in the country
+ Technically absorbing singletrack on the Hardrock Trail
+ The skills area is one of best around for technically able riders
− No real hills – making for easy riding, but meaning there are few descents
− Blue and green trails have a very high proportion of forest road
− Limited facilities but more available in Dalbeattie village

Directions

Head south west from Dumfries on the A711 for 13 miles to Dalbeattie. Once in Dalbeattie, follow the A710. The car park is on your left a short way south of the town.

Grid Ref: NX 836590   **Sat Nav:** DG5 4QU

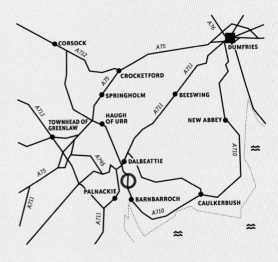

The trails

IRONHASH TRAIL

DISTANCE: 11.5KM	TIME: 1.5–2HRS
EFFORT: 2/5	TECHNICALITY: 2/5

The green-graded Ironhash Trail is just over 11km in length and is a good, fairly flat ride for inexperienced riders. Although the trail follows forest road for most of its length, there are two short sections of singletrack on the route. Both are pretty easy – the first being a well-surfaced, fairly straight trail through the trees and the second being a more natural stretch of open trail – and add a little technical interest to the trail. A gentle trail of decent length, ideal for a relaxed ride.

MOYLE HILL TRAIL

DISTANCE: 14KM	TIME: 1.5–3HRS
EFFORT: 3/5	TECHNICALITY: 2/5

The Moyle Hill Trail is a good choice if you want to get out and cover a reasonable distance and take in some views without encountering any real technical difficulty. It's raised slightly above the surrounding countryside on the side of a hill, so you can see a fair old way, and it uses mainly forest roads. The route does share some of the Hardrock Trail's easier sections of singletrack and there's some low and wide boardwalk (nothing to worry about) near the beginning, but that's about it in terms of technicality. If you're looking for singletrack, pick another route.

Trails continue...

JAMES DYMOND

DALBEATTIE
continued...

HARDROCK TRAIL

DISTANCE: 27KM	**TIME:** 2–4HRS
EFFORT: 3/5	**TECHNICALITY:** 3/5

Characterised by its narrow singletrack and the lumps of granite dotted across the trail, you have to watch your lines on the Hardrock Trail. Winding along rough singletrack and over small rock features, the trail makes its way to the infamous Slab – a steep, 14-metre granite drop. It's far easier than it looks, but there are singletrack options to either side if you're not up for it. More rocky singletrack leads to the Terrible Twins – Dalbeattie's second slab feature. The Twins are smaller and less scary than The Slab but shouldn't be underestimated – they're steeper and trickier to ride. After them, the trail speeds up and heads home via some optional north shore and technical black features. Relatively technical singletrack and easily-to-bottle trail features make this a great ride for the technically adept.

Good to know

There is also an extensive skills area at the beginning of the trails. It doesn't contain any berms or jumps, just tricky rocky slabs and ridges. The rock is grippy, but that doesn't mean it's easy: there are some hard climbs and tricky corners to tackle, as well as some rocky ridges with gaps bridged by north shore and two steep slabs to roll down – if you dare.

HAMISH McCOOL

DRUMLANRIG

Centre pros and cons
+ Fantastic winding, rooty singletrack
+ Constant attention means the trails stay in top shape
+ A wide range of trails means there's something for everyone
+ Drumlanrig is all about progression. A complete beginner can start on the tarmac trails and work their way up
+ The only trail centre in the UK to come complete with a museum dedicated to the history of the bicycle!

Directions
From Dumfries, take the A76 north towards Kilmarnock for 17 miles (27.5km). After passing through Thornhill, Drumlanrig Castle is signposted. Turn left onto minor roads and follow the signs.

Grid Ref: NX 852993   **Sat Nav:** DG3 4AQ

About the centre
In 1839, Kirkpatrick MacMillan wheeled the world's first bicycle out of a smithy near Drumlanrig Castle. Now, many years later, Drumlanrig must be the only 17th Century castle anywhere to have superb woodland trails weaving through the woods a few hundred metres from its front door. This unusual state of affairs has come about thanks to the Drumlanrig Estate and Rik Alsop, who runs the bike shop in the castle's courtyard and makes sure nobody's cutting corners on his singletrack. There are trails here for everybody, beginning with tarmac loops and progressing gradually through easy off-road trails to singletrack and rooty horror shows.

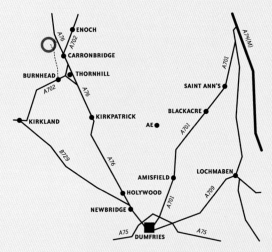

The trails

THE POLICY

DISTANCE: 3KM	TIME: 0.5–1HR
EFFORT: 1/5	TECHNICALITY: 1/5

BURNSANDS

DISTANCE: 13KM	TIME: 1–2HRS
EFFORT: 2/5	TECHNICALITY: 1/5

ROCKING STONE

DISTANCE: 5KM	TIME: 0.5–1HR
EFFORT: 1/5	TECHNICALITY: 2/5

LOW GARDENS

DISTANCE: 8KM	TIME: 0.75–1.5HRS
EFFORT: 1/5	TECHNICALITY: 2/5

Drumlanrig's green routes are spot on for complete novices and young children to get out on their bikes, have some fun and improve their riding. First up is The Policy – a short route, entirely on tarmac, that you could ride with stabilisers. You can then build some fitness with the longer Burnsands route. Still on tarmac, it's on quiet public roads and has a few gentle climbs. After this, you can move off-road on the Rocking Stone and Low Gardens routes. The first drops gently down through the woods on wide easy trails before returning to the car park on the estate's roads. The last route heads out on tarmac, but heads home on dirt, with a slightly steeper and more varied trail surface. Combine these last two routes and you have an easy blue-graded route.

COPY CAT

DISTANCE: 9KM	TIME: 0.5–1HR
EFFORT: 2/5	TECHNICALITY: 2/5

So, you've built up a little riding experience and want to push things a little… Try the Copy Cat. It shadows Drumlanrig's red route, running along some of that route's easier singletrack in places and, in others, hovering nearby on wide tracks. If you feel comfortable on them and enjoy the narrow, twisting trails, the 'Copy Cat' nature of the route allows you to nip off the blue and onto the red itself for a few more tight corners. If you're happy as you are, stick to the blue, have a little rest on the easier sections and save your energy for the next singletrack run. It's all about progression!

SECRET FOREST

DISTANCE: 11KM	TIME: 0.5–1.5HRS
EFFORT: 3/5	TECHNICALITY: 2/5

Technically easy, this is a route for those of us who like getting out on our bikes, tackling some hard climbs and enjoying the views. Initially following easy dirt trails, the route climbs, steeply at times, through the woods for a fair distance, emerging onto a quiet tarmac lane above the estate. This stretch is fairly long, but high up with some decent views, and leads around the top of the woods. Dropping back in, the trail loses height pretty rapidly on more easy dirt trails – although there's plenty of scope for winding up the speed to make things more exciting.

Trails continue…

DRUMLANRIG
continued...

THE OLD SCHOOL

DISTANCE: 15.5KM	**TIME:** 1.5–2.5HRS
EFFORT: 3/5	**TECHNICALITY:** 3/5

This is classic woodland singletrack. Natural-feeling dirt trails tuck and turn between the trees, bringing a lovely flowing feel to The Old School, although you definitely have to pick your lines carefully to keep that smooth momentum going. Why? Roots. They're everywhere on this trail. If you're riding well, they spice the trail up nicely, forcing you to stay awake and keep your eyes open. Hit the trail when things aren't going well however, and you'll struggle! A fairly hard trail technically, the constant urge to sprint the singletrack, ducking around turns and lifting the bike over roots wears you down physically, especially when compared to the smoothly-groomed trails of many trail centres. But then, it's the perfect antidote to those trails, and they do say that variety is the spice of life.

HELL'S CAULDRON

DISTANCE: 23.5KM (INC. RED)	**TIME:** 1.5–3HRS
EFFORT: 4/5	**TECHNICALITY:** 4/5

If you thought the previous trail was rooty, look away now! A series of extensions to The Old School, Hell's Cauldron turns the difficulty up a notch or two. The climbs are bigger and steeper, the corners are tighter (watch out for the TTT – Too Tight Turn, which had to be made more obvious as riders weren't spotting the sharp flick back on themselves!) and the roots are bigger. You can expect rooty drops, steep descents and corners where the biggest roots sit exactly where you don't want them. Highly technical, hard work and great fun.

Good to know

- You can buy an up-to-date map of Drumlanrig's trails at Rik's Bike Shed.
- At time of going to print, it costs £4 to ride at Drumlanrig. This is a charge levied by the estate, without whose money and permission the trails wouldn't have been built. Yes, you are in Scotland and can legally ride virtually anywhere but here, no money = no more singletrack.
- There's also an 'uplift' service into the nearby hills if you want to explore the surrounding area without putting in the effort. Call Rik's shop for details.

© MBR (MOUNTAIN BIKE RIDER) MAGAZINE

FIRE TOWER TRAIL

About the centre

Lying a fair way from major cities and the most popular riding destinations, the Fire Tower Trail near Lochgilphead is much quieter than most trail centres. Although there's not enough riding on the trail itself to fill a weekend, the trail is situated within beautiful countryside with some great riding nearby and Fort William only a two or three hour drive away. The trail itself is best suited to intermediate riders, who will be challenged by the many black-graded trail features and appreciate the singletrack linking them, and more advanced riders who will hit the technical sections hard and fast and come out grinning.

Centre pros and cons

+ Lots of engaging trail features to tackle; steep drops, rocky outcrops and wall-like climbs
+ Good signage gives you the direction and distance to trail features; make up your own route
+ Solid red route with black graded options to play around on
− No facilities (head into Lochgilphead)
− Singletrack flow isn't up there with the best

Directions

Take the A82 north from Glasgow, turning onto the A83 at Tarbet, following signs for Campbeltown. Just under 50 picturesque miles later, go through Lochgilphead and turn north onto the A816. Bear right (still on the A816) when the road forks and then immediately turn right onto a forest road. The car park is on your right, after the buildings.

Grid Ref: NR 851909   **Sat Nav:** PA31 8SJ

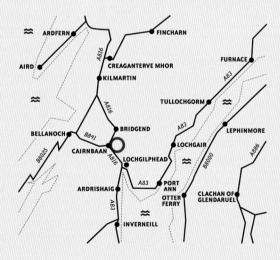

The trails

FIRE TOWER TRAIL	
DISTANCE: 19KM	**TIME:** 1.5–2.5HRS
EFFORT: 3/5	**TECHNICALITY:** 3/5

After warming up on a fire road climb and a scorching little singletrack descent, the trail begins a long drag uphill, initially on forest road but then on well-surfaced singletrack. Pick your way along the rock outcrop that forms the optional Fire Tower Loop and blaze off down the trail to the steep but rollable Quarry Drop. More fire road brings you to the bottom of Murder Hill, a pretty intense singletrack climb that'll sear your lungs and leave your legs burning. Things soon hot up with a fast descent around rough berms and jumps before cooling off in the Water Splash – which should be avoided when in spate. More good singletrack leads you to a lengthy, but easy, stretch of north shore and the end of the trail.

Good to know

You can start the Fire Tower Trail from three car parks:

1 Achnabreac (see main directions).

2 Near Kilmichael Glassery (continue along the A816 past the Achnabreac car park, and turn right into Bridgend. About a kilometre further along, just after crossing the river, turn right onto a forest track to a car park. **Grid Ref: NR 851 909**).

3 From Lochgilphead (park in town and head for the hospital on Blarbuie Road. Go past it and ride up to the golf course. You can access the trail from here. **Grid Ref: NR 877 889**).

📷 HOWARD COTTON

FORT WILLIAM
The Witch's Trails

AT A GLANCE
BEGINNERS: 1/3   **INTERMEDIATE:** 2/3   **ADVANCED:** 3/3

FACILITIES

 Gondola uplift for Downhill course

THE TRAILS
Cour Loop .... Blue 19km
10 Under The Ben .... Red 16.5km
World Champs .... Red 8.5km
Downhill / 4X .... Orange .. 2.7km/c.500m

NEAREST BIKE SHOP
Off Beat Bikes, Fort William – t: 01397 704 008
Nevis Cycles, Inverlochy – t: 01397 705 555

MORE INFORMATION
w: www.nevisrange.co.uk   **w:** www.ridefortwilliam.co.uk
w: www.fortwilliamworldcup.co.uk

Centre pros and cons

+ Quite literally world class trails
+ Two good, constantly changing red routes
+ Long, easy-riding and scenic blue route
+ Gondola uplift provides easy access to the DH track
+ What a location!

Directions

Head north from Fort William on the A82 towards Inverness.

The Nevis Range is clearly signposted on your right after 3 miles.

Grid Ref: NN 171774   **Sat Nav:** PH33 6SW

About the centre

Fort William is the only UK trail centre to have achieved
international fame. The Mountain Bike World Cup has been
held on the trails there since 2002 and, in 2007, Fort William
staged the World Championships. It has picked up numerous
awards for these races, including the riders' award for their
favourite event. Not bad... but it gets better – the racecourses
are open to the public. You can ride the technical XC loop,
launch yourself down the 4X course or see how much faster
professional downhill racers are than you on one of the longest
and roughest courses on the international circuit.

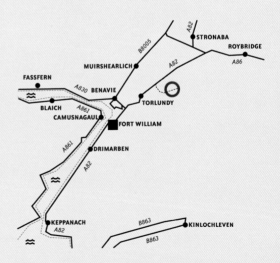

The trails

COUR LOOP

DISTANCE: 18KM	TIME: 1.5–3HRS
EFFORT: 3/5	TECHNICALITY: 2/5

The Cour Loop is a scenic route beginning from the Nevis Range centre and following wide, well-surfaced tracks through the Leanachan forest. A reasonable amount of climbing takes you up onto the Puggy Line – an old narrow gauge railway line – before descending through woodland towards the River Cour. Well within the capabilities of most reasonably fit riders, the Cour Loop is a good choice if you're looking for a technically straightforward ride of decent length with some great views.

10 UNDER THE BEN

DISTANCE: 16.5KM	TIME: 1–2HRS
TECHNICALITY: 4/5	EFFORT: 3/5

Regularly used for endurance racing, the 10 Under the Ben trail starts on singletrack, with a few turns and some steep drops to roll. This is followed by a long stretch of easy riding on wide tracks, which luckily, are fast in places and so reasonably enjoyable. The course then swings downhill on good woodland singletrack to Nessie – a steep rocky descent around a corner. Good fun, but way, way harder than the rest of the route. The return to the car park is flatter, with some technical and some fast sections. Overall, this is a slightly confused route – the first half is well-suited to less-advanced riders, but even international racers have been caught out by Nessie! Good fun though.

WORLD CHAMPS

DISTANCE: 8.5KM	TIME: 1–2HRS
EFFORT: 4/5	TECHNICALITY: 3/5

Tough for a red route, the World Champs trail follows the usual one climb and one descent format found at many trail centres. The difference is that here, both are longer and steeper than usual. Right from the start, the trail climbs steeply and soon hits singletrack. It's well surfaced and not technically difficult, but goes on and on and on! It's worth the effort though, as nothing's wasted on the way down. Initially fast and bermed, the trail soon tightens and becomes more technical, with tight corners and rocks coming at you. Hard to ride fast and smoothly, it feels awesome when you hit a section well.

Trails continue...

FORT WILLIAM
The Witch's Trails continued...

JOHN COEFIELD

DOWNHILL AND 4X

DISTANCE: 2.7KM / c.500M	**TIME:** 5 MINS (PROS) / N/A
EFFORT: 4/5 / 2/5	**TECHNICALITY:** 5/5 / 4/5

It would be pretty hard to miss the downhill and 4X courses –
they finish in the centre of the car park. The downhill in
particular is Fort William's crowning glory. It's long, rough and
hard. With easy gondola access (check websites – seasonal
opening only), the top section rattles over rock gardens before
the trail drops into the woods. It doesn't ease up though – there
may be fractionally fewer rocks but there are roots and mud to
contend with. The lower section is fast, with big jumps. A hard
course. The 4X has recently been extended to a good length
and contains some sizeable jumps – making it scarier than the
DH in many ways.

Good to know

- You can ride out to the trails from Fort William – it's not too
  far and there are cycle tracks for much of the way.
- If you fancy seeing the world's best in action, go to
  www.fortwilliamworldcup.co.uk for all the information
  you'll ever need.

HOWARD COTTON

JOHN COEFIELD

GLENTRESS
7stanes

AT A GLANCE
BEGINNERS: 3/3   **INTERMEDIATE:** 3/3   **ADVANCED:** 3/3

FACILITIES

THE TRAILS
Green	Green	4.5km
Blue	Blue	16km
Red	Red	19km
Black	Black	30km
Freeride Park	Orange	N/A

NEAREST BIKE SHOP
The Hub in the Forest (on site) – t: 01721 721 736

MORE INFORMATION
w: www.7stanes.gov.uk   w: www.thehubintheforest.co.uk

Centre pros and cons

+ Brilliantly hard, technical singletrack riding
+ Good singletrack trails for every level of rider
+ Extensive bike park
+ Good facilities, including a great café
− Gets busy, understandably

Directions

From Edinburgh, get onto the ring road and head south on the A703 or A701, following signs for Peebles. The two roads merge and then separate – take the A703 towards Peebles. Once there, turn east on the A72. The trails are easily spotted on the left 2 miles outside the town.

Grid Ref: NT 284397   **Sat Nav:** EH45 8NB

About the centre

Glentress is a trail centre for mountain bikers. There are no forest road routes here and no long, easy rides. Instead, each and every trail is about enjoying the technical interest of the ride. The green route is approximately fifty-percent singletrack. The blue mixes elements of the red with its own sweeping trails. The red is in places rough and ready and in others fast and jumpy. Meanwhile, the long black route is almost entirely technical singletrack. Add a great café in the shape of The Hub in the Forest and it becomes clear why Glentress is among the busiest trail centres in the UK.

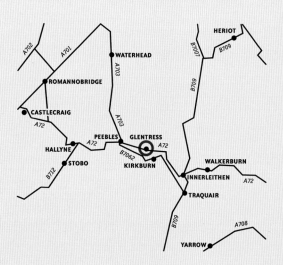

The trails

GREEN

DISTANCE: 4.5KM	TIME: 0.5–1HR
EFFORT: 1/5	TECHNICALITY: 2/5

En route to the green route is Glentress's green-graded **Skills Area**. Containing a decent amount of singletrack, plenty of corners, small drops and climbs this is a lot of fun. It's also a good way to become a better rider, as each 'challenge' is accompanied by a small sign to coach you through it. Ride this loop and then head out onto the green route, where you'll find wide, smooth singletrack that drops, climbs and generally weaves through the trees. Throw in a few picnic benches, a couple of viewpoints and you have a great ride. Proof that easy riding doesn't have to be boring!

BLUE

DISTANCE: 16KM	TIME: 1–2.5HRS
EFFORT: 3/5	TECHNICALITY: 3/5

Glentress's blue route has a lot going for it. A definite notch up from the green, the blue route is characterised by its fast and flowing singletrack. Sweeping corners and jumps encourage you to wind up the speed and the good, solid trail surface makes it easy to do so. If you want a little more, the trail shadows the red route, so pick up a map and you'll have a few options for heading along some more technical singletrack. One last thing – start from the lower car park. It might be a slog uphill, but the returning singletrack descents are the best on the route!

Trails continue...

[📷] © MBR (MOUNTAIN BIKE RIDER) MAGAZINE

[📷] © MBR (MOUNTAIN BIKE RIDER) MAGAZINE

GLENTRESS
continued...

RED

DISTANCE: 19KM	TIME: 1.5–3HRS
EFFORT: 3/5	TECHNICALITY: 4/5

Home of the Spooky Woods descent, this is one of the most enjoyable trails around. It's not a tight or twisty trail, focusing instead on speed. The aforementioned Spooky Woods is the perfect example, packing in a silly amount of jumps and bermed corners before the trail careers off into the next singletrack section at high speed. Don't go thinking that this is another perfectly smooth and groomed trail though – it's rough and it's cut up – a proper mountain bike trail. To get the most out of it you need to be confident and aggressive with the bumps (or just ride a full suspension bike and glide over them). One of the best trails in the UK.

BLACK

DISTANCE: 30KM	TIME: 2.5–5HRS
EFFORT: 5/5	TECHNICALITY: 4/5

This is a 30km route. More importantly, this is a 30km route with close to 24km of singletrack. And that's 24km of superb, hard singletrack. There are rocky climbs, switchback descents, and swooping dirt sections. In places you'll be manualling through compressions and in others you'll be hanging on as you rattle over rock gardens. There's Deliverance – a very long, flowing trail. There's the Ewok Village, with its north shore and there's Britney Spears, with her bermed corners and steep climb. A rough, fast and brilliant trail, but one that will leave you with tired legs, sore hands and, probably, a fair dose of arm-pump. Awesome!

FREERIDE PARK

DISTANCE: N/A	TIME: N/A
EFFORT: 1/5	TECHNICALITY: 4/5

With multiple jump-lines, wallrides and north shore, Glentress's Freeride Park is a popular spot. The jumps are predominantly table tops of varying sizes, so there's plenty of scope to start small and build up. There are two wall rides (which you can either ride or you can't), and a box at the end that you can jump onto and off. There are easier lines for those wanting a little play, but plenty of scope for those who want to give it large.

Good to know

- The blue, red and black trails can be started from either the lower or higher car parks. Go for the lower – it may mean more climbing, but the returning piece of singletrack, Falla Brae, is something you won't want to miss.
- There are signed shortcuts back at various points along the routes in case things get a bit much for you.

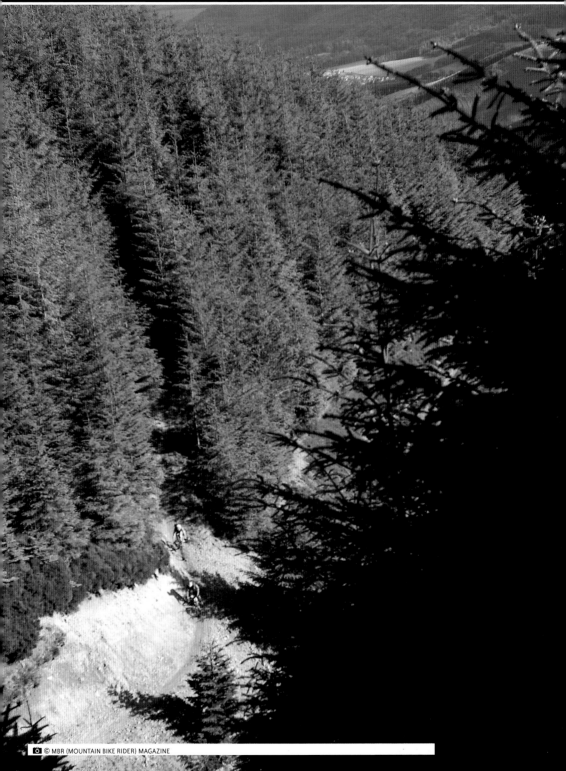

GLENTROOL
7stanes

About the centre

Glentrool is unique among the 7 Stanes in that it has no trails above a blue grade and no technical singletrack. Instead, it has two easy green and one blue-graded trails and an ungraded beast of a route that traces a 58 km loop through the surrounding countryside. The green and blue trails contain a nice mixture of singletrack and wider trails and are a good choice for those wanting an easy but enjoyable ride. The monster loop is a better option if you're feeling fit and like your rides to be Big Days Out in the countryside.

Centre pros and cons

+ Great for long rides out into the countryside
+ Good for inexperienced riders, with three routes to choose between
- No technical singletrack (but then again, there was never meant to be!)

Directions

From Dumfries, take the A75 west to Newton Stewart. In Newton Stewart, turn right onto the A714 for about 8 miles, before turning right to Glentrool Village. The centre is up a small lane on your right just after the village.

Grid Ref: NX 371787   **Sat Nav:** NEWTON STEWART

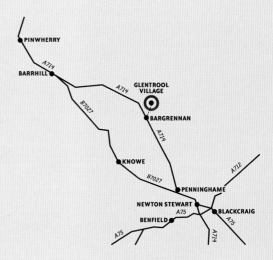

The trails

PULNAGASHEL GLEN

DISTANCE: 6KM	TIME: 0.5–1.5HRS
EFFORT: 1/5	TECHNICALITY: 2/5

Striking a good balance between forest road and singletrack, this is a fun route that should be well within the capabilities of everyone, including younger riders. It leaves the car park on wide, easy singletrack before heading gently uphill on forest roads and more narrow(ish) trails for a relatively long, but gradual climb. Some fun singletrack traversing around sweeping corners follows before a forest road descent returns to the visitor centre. A pleasant, enjoyable ride.

PALGOWAN

DISTANCE: 14KM	TIME: 1–2.5HRS
EFFORT: 2/5	TECHNICALITY: 1/5

Despite sharing its first two or three kilometres with the similarly-graded Pulnagashel Glen trail, the Palgowan route has a completely different nature. Peeling away from that route, it contains no singletrack, but follows forest roads and farm tracks through woodland and open countryside. There's no technical difficulty, but more distance is covered and there's a lot more to see. It can get exposed in places, so pick your day carefully. This is a nice route for introducing younger or less experienced riders to 'proper', rather than manmade, mountain biking.

GREEN TORR

DISTANCE: 9KM	TIME: 1–2HRS
EFFORT: 2/5	TECHNICALITY: 2/5

Climbing away from the final descent of the Pulnagashel Glen route, the Green Torr isn't a great deal harder. Sharing the majority of its length with the former route, it follows forest roads to gain extra height and some fine views before heading downhill to the visitor centre. The descent is on smooth singletrack. There are no tricky obstacles, roots and rocks in the way and the gently-bermed corners are easy to ride. It is both steeper and faster than the green route, but not by too much, so, if you're riding that route and reach the point where the two split feeling confident, why not give the blue a whirl?

BIG COUNTRY ROUTE

DISTANCE: 58KM	TIME: 3.5–7HRS
EFFORT: 5/5	TECHNICALITY: 2/5

Ae is jumpy, Dalbeattie is rocky and Kirroughtree flows. Glentrool is all about long days out in the hills. The Big Country Route is a sizeable ride out into the Galloway hills on stone and dirt tracks and quiet lanes. There's no singletrack or technical riding, but it's a long way around and there are some big hills to conquer. En-route, you'll pass through woodlands, ride past quarries and stone carvings and be shown some expansive views out over lochs and hills. This is the route to choose if you want a full day out appreciating the countryside from your saddle.

GOLSPIE

AT A GLANCE
BEGINNERS: 1/3   **INTERMEDIATE:** 2/3   **ADVANCED:** 3/3

FACILITIES
Shops in Golspie

THE TRAILS
Blue Trail .... Blue 6.5km
Red Trail .... Red 7.5km
Black Trail .... Black 13.6km

MORE INFORMATION
w: www.highlandwildcat.com

About the centre
Currently the most northerly trail centre in the UK, the Highland Wildcat trails were built on the slopes of Ben Bhraggie with community funding and the help of trail builder Pete Laing. Starting at sea level, the routes climb towards the summit of the Ben (great views out over the Moray Firth) via one of the longest singletrack climbs – and descents – at any trail centre in the country. Offering a pleasant blue, exhilarating red and one of the hardest black routes in the country, Golspie is a centre able to cater for most mountain bikers.

Centre pros and cons
+ Good choice of great trails
+ Rocky black route adds technical and jumpy challenges – and a long, long singletrack descent
+ Fast and swoopy red is great fun
+ Pleasant blue route contains some good, but easy singletrack
+ Fairly quiet
− Locations this far north get a battering in winter – which means snow-covered trails and cold toes when riding

Directions
From Inverness, head north on the A9 for 50 miles to Golspie. Either park in the town centre (there's a car park on the left of the main road as you head north), or turn left, passing the entrance to the town centre car park, and continue over the roundabout and under the bridge to a higher car park.

Grid Ref: NC 828005   **Sat Nav:** GOLSPIE

The trails

BLUE TRAIL

DISTANCE: 6.5KM	TIME: 0.5–1.5HRS
EFFORT: 2/5	TECHNICALITY: 2/5

Golspie's blue route is a fun ride. Park out of town and climb some snaking singletrack to join the red and black routes. More climbing on more snaking singletrack carries you up onto the hillside for some good views out towards the sea and some forest road bashing. That done with, it's back onto the same singletrack you climbed earlier. Predictably, it's more enjoyable in this direction and deposits you back in the car park with a big smile. Watch out for riders coming in the opposite direction.

RED TRAIL

DISTANCE: 7.5KM	TIME: 1–2HRS
EFFORT: 3/5	TECHNICALITY: 3/5

The trail kicks off, unavoidably, with a climb. Luckily, it's on singletrack with a smooth and sandy surface. The odd rock step here and there keeps things interesting, as do the snaking hairpins. Once up, a quick forest road traverse leads to the descent. This is a fast and flowing affair, carving around berms, over jumps (which are fairly large for a red XC trail) and off drops which, although rollable, will fire you some way down the trail if you hit them at speed. Guaranteed to put a grin on your face, no matter how fast you ride.

BLACK TRAIL

DISTANCE: 13.6KM	TIME: 1.5–3HRS
EFFORT: 4/5	TECHNICALITY: 5/5

Let's see... the longest singletrack descent in Scotland... awesome technical climbing... jumps, drops, rocky outcrops... decided yet? An extension to the red, this is one of the hardest trails in the UK. You'd better be good at climbing, because the rocky steps and squeezes will get you if you're not. You'd better be able to jump, as you will get airborne on the fast top section. And you'd better know how to handle a bike, because the rocky sections are tight, steep and tricky. There are shortcuts – one of which, 'Treeline', is a great technical climb – and there are chicken runs but think about it, you've not come all this way to take easy lines, have you?

Good to know

To ride the blue, you'll either need to park in the town and follow the red route until you spot the blue waymarks, or, better, drive north out of Golspie and then turn sharp left up a tiny lane signed 'Backies' under a railway bridge. Follow this to a car park up on your right (**Grid Ref: NC 838014**).

📷 HOWARD COTTON

INNERLEITHEN
7stanes

AT A GLANCE
BEGINNERS: 0/3   **INTERMEDIATE:** 3/3   **ADVANCED:** 3/3

FACILITIES

THE TRAILS
Traquair XC .... Red (with black options) .. 18km
Downhill .... Orange .... N/A

NEAREST BIKE SHOP
Alpine Bikes, Innerleithen – t: 01896 830 880

MORE INFORMATION
w: www.7stanes.gov.uk   **w:** www.upliftscotland.com

About the centre

Just down the road from Glentress, Innerleithen is a venue for the more experienced rider. Lacking the blue and green routes of its neighbour, Innerleithen has only one XC trail – the red/black-graded Traquair XC. As with Glentress's top-end routes, this is a hard-riding and technical trail, best-suited to people who can ride it that way. Unlike Glentress, the trail is relatively quiet, but this doesn't extend to the car park, which is often packed, as Innerleithen is a popular and busy downhilling venue, with several tracks running down the hill and a regular uplift service.

Centre pros and cons

\+ Technical singletrack trail with red and black options

\+ Loads of downhill trails

\+ Good location; close to Glentress and plenty more
natural riding

\- Nothing for beginners

\- Limited facilities but Innerleithen village close by

Directions

From Edinburgh, get onto the ring road and head south on the A703 or A701, following signs for Peebles. The two roads merge and then separate – take the A703 towards Peebles. Once there, turn east on the A72, pass Glentress on your left and continue along the main road to Innerleithen. Once in the village, turn right following signs to Traquair. The car park is on your left at the T-junction.

Grid Ref: NT 336357   **Sat Nav:** EH44 6PD

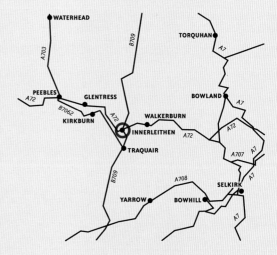

The trails

TRAQUAIR XC	
DISTANCE: 18KM	TIME: 1.5–4HRS
EFFORT: 4/5	TECHNICALITY: 4/5

The Traquair XC rewards confidence. Beginning with a long climb, it winds up through woods onto rocky moorland. Stop to admire the (extensive) views and then blast onto the first singletrack descent. Instantly fast, the trail gains momentum as it flows over jumps and drops. Then comes the technical Plora Craig, with singletrack snaking rapidly through the trees before abruptly hitting black-graded rock gardens. If you need it, there's a more flowing red option that bypasses the hardest sections. Last, but most certainly not least, is Caddon Bank. Fast and steep with massive berms, big drops and rows of doubles, this is Glentress's Spooky Woods on steroids and you'll need to attack the trail to ride it well. A fine end to a great ride.

DOWNHILL	
DISTANCE: N/A	TIME: N/A
EFFORT: 3/5	TECHNICALITY: 5/5

Innerleithen = downhill. A popular and regular race venue with four main tracks (and numerous other lines) and a regular uplift service, Innerleithen is one of the UK's premier downhill venues – and has been for over a decade. The main tracks are the big, hard and fast Matador, the tight and natural Gold and Cresta Runs, splattered with roots and off-camber traverses, and Make or Brake – a high-speed run over jumps and berms. All excellent runs. All definitely worth riding.

Good to know

See **www.upliftscotland.com** for details of the regular uplift service that runs virtually every weekend. It's also probably worth checking to see if there are any downhill races on before a visit, although Glentress is just up the road if you can't ride at Innerleithen because an event is taking place.

HAMISH McCOOL

DOUG INGLIS

JEDBURGH

About the centre

The Jedburgh Forest trails are waymarked routes that take you through the surrounding countryside on predominantly natural trails. If it's miles of carefully-built, all-weather singletrack you're after, you'd be better off hopping over to one of the nearby 7 Stanes centres. What's on offer here is a nice variety of trails, from narrow singletrack to wide farm tracks and grassy fields. Although the waymarking is reasonable, it's worth taking a map and some information on the route with you, just in case you miss a turning or want to take a shortcut home. The full Justice Trail is a big ride, so you'll need to be well-prepared before tackling it.

Centre pros and cons

+ A great halfway house between natural and manmade riding
+ Some great sections of riding
+ Ride the Lanton Loop for brilliant, if short, natural singletrack
+ The full Justice Trail is a big, varied ride
− Some of the riding suffers from use by horses
− It's hard to find the start of the routes

Directions

Jedburgh is on the A68, which runs between Newcastle and Edinburgh (roughly 55 miles from Newcastle and 45 from Edinburgh). Once in Jedburgh, turn into the town and park in the main car park beside the Tourist Information Office.

Grid Ref: NT 651203   **Sat Nav:** TD8 6BE

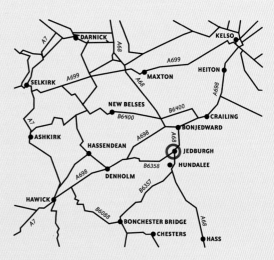

The trails

DERE STREET DASH

DISTANCE: 10.5KM	TIME: 1–2HRS
EFFORT: 2/5	TECHNICALITY: 2/5

Once you've found the start of the route, the Dere Street Dash is an enjoyable ride. Using mainly quiet roads and wide tracks, it can get muddy in places, but is generally a decent all-weather bet. The route starts with a fair bit of climbing on tarmac and easy trails, before dropping down and onto a short section of wide, natural singletrack and finishing up alongside the main road. Whilst not ideal for children, this is a reasonable route for inexperienced mountain bikers.

LANTON LOOP

DISTANCE: 6.5KM	TIME: 0.5–1HR
EFFORT: 2/5	TECHNICALITY: 2/5

Ooh – woodland singletrack! After a quick spin up and along easy tracks, the trail turns a corner and gets progressively narrower. Gently-kinked corners and a natural berm or two make for a fast, bike-flicking ride through the trees. The odd root could catch you out, but keep your eyes open and they just add to the fun. Unfortunately, the trail cuts up a bit in the winter and is pretty popular with horse riders – not a great combination. So, the summer brings speedy fun, the winter brings mud (and sliding fun). Again, not great for young children, but for everyone else, it's a blast.

JUSTICE TRAIL

DISTANCE: 40KM	TIME: 2.5–5HRS
EFFORT: 4/5	TECHNICALITY: 2/5

Heading out along the Dere Street Dash, the Justice Trail then climbs up to join the Lanton Loop. Iif you want to charge along that route's singletrack (you do!), you'll have to ride it in its entirety before rejoining the Justice Trail. From there, this route bashes out cross-country across some muddy tracks to some pretty uninspiring riding across tussocky fields. Keep going, there's some good, woody singletrack to come in Swinnie Plantation before a fast spin home on good tracks. The route can get muddy in places, especially in some of the singletrack sections, but go in summer when the flowers are out and the trails are dry, and you should have a good ride.

Good to know

- Start the Justice Trail and Dere Street Dash from the car park beside Jedburgh Tourist Information office. You can pick up route maps here as well.
- To begin the rides, turn right out of the car park and cross the main road onto Duck Row. Cross the bridge and climb to the left. Go straight ahead at the crossroads and bear left onto a dirt track. You'll soon see the signs.
- For the Lanton Loop, turn left out of the car park, go straight ahead over the crossroads and take the first right. Bear left at the T-junction and climb the hill to the woods, where there are a few parking spots.

KIRKHILL

AT A GLANCE
BEGINNERS: 3/5   **INTERMEDIATE:** 3/5   **ADVANCED:** 3/5

FACILITIES

THE TRAILS
Blue .... Blue 12km
Fun Park .... Blue (with red features) .. 2km

NEAREST BIKE SHOP
Alpine Bikes, Aberdeen – t: 01224 211 455
Edinburgh Cycle Co-op, Aberdeen – t: 01224 632 994

MORE INFORMATION
w: www.forestry.gov.uk

About the centre

Sitting just outside Aberdeen, the Forestry Commission-owned Kirkhill Forest is a popular destination for local riders. There are two waymarked trails – a relatively easy blue loop on good tracks, and a purpose built 'fun park' trail. The former is a good choice for fitter novices and the fun park, although enjoyable for better riders, is also aimed at less-experienced cyclists. There are, however, some great natural trails tucked away in the forest (it's these that make the forest so popular with the locals) and which are more suited to those seeking good singletrack. All in all, good waymarked trails for beginners, good hidden stuff for the more adventurous.

Centre pros and cons

+ The Fun Park is close to the car park and is good fun for decent riders while remaining ridable by beginners
+ Lots of fantastic singletrack tucked away in the forest (not marked)
+ The blue loop is a good way to explore and look out for new trails, or to have a gentle ride in some pleasant woodland
− Not much waymarked singletrack

Directions

From Aberdeen, head north on the A96 towards Inverness. The forest is on the right-hand side of the dual carriageway, about 8 miles from Aberdeen, and a short distance before the turning/roundabout for Blackburn.

Grid Ref: NJ 855115   **Sat Nav:** BLACKBURN

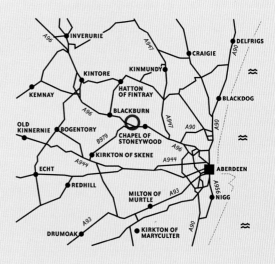

The trails

BLUE	
DISTANCE: 12KM	**TIME:** 0.75–1.5HRS
EFFORT: 2/5	**TECHNICALITY:** 1/5

A circular loop around a plateau at the top of Kirkhill on good, wide tracks, this isn't a technical ride. It's not particularly hard work either, although there is a bit of a climb involved. Before more experienced riders write the trail off though, take a look at the north and south spurs, which can be used to link the trail to the car parks at either end of the forest. These, particularly the south spur, are far more entertaining, with some steep slopes, tight turns and rocks and roots to contend with. A quick lap of the loop will also reveal a large number of enticing singletrack trails running into the pine forest on either side of the trail…

FUN PARK	
DISTANCE: 2KM	**TIME:** 0.25HR
EFFORT: 2/5	**TECHNICALITY:** 2/5

As you'd guess, the Fun Park is fast and exciting, dropping downhill around berms and over jumps. What makes it unique is that it is much easier than many similar trails, it is right beside the car park and it can be accessed either from the blue loop or via its own, easy climb. Importantly, it's not particularly steep, meaning that you can get up to a fair pace with a bit of pedalling, or roll down at a much lower speed, if that's what you'd prefer. Everything is rollable and well made, meaning that this is an ideal way for less experienced riders to have a go at this style of riding.

HOWARD COTTON

KIRROUGHTREE

7stanes

AT A GLANCE
BEGINNERS: 4/5   **INTERMEDIATE:** 5/5   **ADVANCED:** 5/5

FACILITIES

THE TRAILS
Bargaly Wood .... Green 6km
Larg Hill .... Blue 10km
Doon Hill Extension .... Blue 4km
The Twister .... Red 17km
Black Craigs .... Black 31km
.... (inc. Red route)

NEAREST BIKE SHOP
The Break Pad (on site) – t: 01671 401 303

MORE INFORMATION
w: www.7stanes.gov.uk

Centre pros and cons
+ Flow!
+ The Twister – 17km of some of the best red-graded singletrack anywhere
+ The incredibly grippy granite of McMoab on the black route
+ A great blue option taking in some of the easier red singletrack

Directions
From Dumfries, take the A75 west towards Newton Stewart. The turning for Kirroughtree is a minor on the right about 4 miles short of Newton Stewart. After turning, take the first left and follow the lane to the centre.

Grid Ref: NX 452644   **Sat Nav:** DG8 7BE

About the centre
Many riders rate Kirroughtree as their favourite trail centre. Set in Galloway Forest, the largest wooded area in the UK, it's in the right location. With carefully-crafted, yet natural-feeling singletrack and awesome natural trail features, it has the riding and, with the nicest-feeling and -flowing singletrack of any trail centre, it's got that special something that sets it above the rest. Set a short distance away from the 'clump' of trails around Dumfries, it is unquestionably worth making the trip over to check it out. There's no way you'll be disappointed.

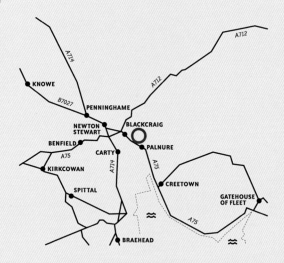

The trails

BARGALY WOOD	
DISTANCE: 6KM	**TIME:** 0.5–1HR
EFFORT: 1/5	**TECHNICALITY:** 1/5

Kirroughtree's Bargaly Wood trail is a short, family-oriented route. Although there's a very short section of easy singletrack, the route otherwise sticks entirely to tarmac and well-surfaced trails. It's worth noting that there is a fair bit of riding along public roads – they're (very) minor and quiet, but you'll still need to keep an eye out for cars. As it's set on the fringes of the Galloway Forest, the surroundings are pleasant, making this an enjoyable ride. If you want more of a 'mountain bike' ride, try the 2km blue-graded 'Taster' singletrack loop.

LARG HILL	
DISTANCE: 10KM	**TIME:** 1–2HRS
DOON HILL EXTENSION	
DISTANCE: 4KM	**TIME:** 0.5HR
EFFORT: 2/5	**TECHNICALITY:** 2/5

That they share some of The Twister's beautifully flowing singletrack doesn't do Kirroughtree's blue routes any harm whatsoever. The trail begins with the Larg Hill loop. Following the same singletrack climb as the red route, it sticks to forest road when the red route moves onto singletrack. This forest road traces a pleasant circuit around Larg Hill before rejoining the red for more fantastically fluid singletrack back to the visitor centre. There is, of course, nothing stopping you following the red trail when it swings off and then rejoining the blue later. The Doon Hill Extension adds a short stretch of singletrack (worth riding), a trip up to a decent viewpoint and a couple of kilometres of forest road.

Trails continue...

© MBR (MOUNTAIN BIKE RIDER) MAGAZINE

KIRROUGHTREE
continued...

THE TWISTER

DISTANCE: 17KM	TIME: 1–2HRS
EFFORT: 3/5	TECHNICALITY: 3/5

You really, really should ride this trail. Bordering on perfection, The Twister somehow manages to blend narrow singletrack trails with tight corners and delicate rocky sections into an effortlessly-flowing whole. Pouring seamlessly from one section to the next, the entire trail seems to merge into one. There are no steep climbs or gradients to break the trail's spell, and technical drops and tight squeezes between trees seem to pass without comment. It's a very natural-feeling trail, devoid of any obviously manmade features and passing through constantly changing woodland. At one point you're through weaving pines, the next, cruising between silver birch. True singletrack nirvana!

BLACK CRAIGS

DISTANCE: 31KM (INC. RED ROUTE)	TIME: 2.5–4HRS
EFFORT: 4/5	TECHNICALITY: 4/5

You must have heard of McMoab. It's a large outcrop of incredibly grippy granite, with painted arrows depicting the best line across its surface. Technical and great fun, it's the dominating feature of the Black Craigs route. It's not, however, the only thing that makes the trail worth riding. Technical rocky features protrude from the singletrack that makes up the route at regular intervals. There are steep slabs to climb and rocky drops to blast off or pick your way down. The trail doesn't flow quite as well as the Twister, but that's not the singletrack's fault – it's more due to the technical difficulty and steep climbs (Heartbreak Hill is possibly the steepest climb at any trail centre). A decent and tricky addition to the red route.

© MBR (MOUNTAIN BIKE RIDER) MAGAZINE

LAGGAN
Wolftrax

Centre pros and cons
+ Relentlessly technical black-graded trail
+ The bike park trail is great for a wide range of riders
+ Popular and technical red route
+ Good facilities

Directions
Laggan is on the A86, which runs between the A82 (Fort William) and the A9 (just south of Aviemore). From Perth, take the A9 north towards Inverness, then turn off onto the A889 towards Dalwhinnie. Turn left onto the A86 at Drumgask. The centre is on your left after about a mile.

Grid Ref: NN 594923   **Sat Nav:** PH20 1BU

About the centre
Since it opened in 2004, Laggan has built itself a big reputation. It's done this by offering trails that cater for every whim and taste – and they're good trails. Starting from the top, there's the infamously difficult black for the technically proficient. There are two flowing trails for XC riders and a great green-graded trail for beginners. In the middle there's the bike park – easy enough to be enjoyed by all, but so much fun to ride fast and hard. Add a decent shop, good café and an uplift service and you've got a great trail centre.

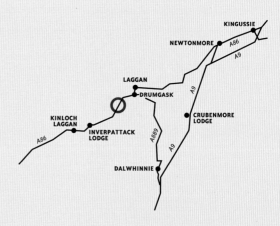

The trails

GREEN

DISTANCE: 5KM	TIME: 1–2HRS
EFFORT: 1/5	TECHNICALITY: 2/5

You've got a couple of options as to how you chose to ride Laggan's green trail. From the centre, a wide and easy route that's built "to Sustrans quality" runs up the valley to the car park at Gorstean, which is an alternative starting point. This track is two-way, so you can make a U-turn and head back to the café for an easy cruise. If you want a bit more excitement, you can head up a gradual climb from the Gorstean car park and follow a shallow singletrack descent instead. Relatively wide, and nice and smooth, it's easy to ride, but there are plenty of twists and turns to ensure that it's never dull.

RED

DISTANCE: 15KM	TIME: 1.5–3HRS
EFFORT: 3/5	TECHNICALITY: 3/5

There are two halves to Laggan's red route, the imaginatively-named 'Upper' red at the top of the hill and, beneath it, the, errr, 'Lower' red. You can ride these as a complete loop, as individual trails or mix them up with the black and bike park runs.

UPPER RED

Sharing a climb with the black, the two trails split at the top of the hill. Initially, it seems that the upper red is going to be a mini version of the black as it rolls between rock slabs. Well, it isn't. Moving out of the trees and onto open ground, the trail smoothes out and widens as speeds increase. Making wide turns it loses height gradually in a relatively repetitive fashion. Nowhere near as technical as the other trails here, it seems a little out of place, although it does add another, easier and faster style of XC riding to the centre. There's the odd optional rock drop, if you want to take them, before the trail re-enters the woods, narrows and rejoins the black run for its final singletrack run to the road.

LOWER RED

You'll want to ride repeat laps of this one! Although far from easy, it's not too hard and flows well throughout much of its length. Good, open singletrack leads from the trailhead down around some nice corners towards the black-graded Air's Rock. You probably noticed this granite slab as you climbed the hill and thought "Woah, that's big". Well, it looks bigger from the top! It's all in your head though, and, having rolled over it, the trail rattles through a couple of rocks gardens and slips into the trees on long, fluid sections of twisting singletrack. A long, downhill section of boardwalk then sends you flying out halfway down the bike park, whose waiting jumps and perfect berms deliver you, grinning, to the café.

Trails continue...

LAGGAN
continued...

BLACK

DISTANCE: 10KM	TIME: 1–2HRS
EFFORT: 3/5	TECHNICALITY: 5/5

And now for something completely different! After a fairly benign singletrack climb, the black reveals its true, jagged nature on the descent. Right from the top, rocky challenge after rocky challenge comes at you. There are rocky slabs to clamber over and drop down. The Devil's Chessboard slaps uneven rock gardens and staircases across the trail. Awkward drops come thick and fast. Even the 'easy' sections are unrelentingly technical and perfectly capable of tripping you up. Don't get too worried though – it's brilliant fun, all just about rideable and a dab-free run is tantalisingly doable.

FUN PARK

DISTANCE: 3.5KM	TIME: 0.5HR
EFFORT: 2/5	TECHNICALITY: 2/5

Once given a blue grade, Laggan's fun park is not technically difficult. It has a wide, smooth, solid surface. There's nothing that you can't roll over and it doesn't drop steeply. It's a trail that anybody can enjoy, but which definitely improves with speed! The trail starts with some long fast corners and tight berms. These soon lengthen, speeds increase and the jumps start to appear. Mainly tabletops, these grow in size as you move down the trail, ending on some fairly sizeable fellows. From the bottom, it's either a long, but easy climb or, if the uplift is running, a lazy drive back to the top.

Good to know

An old Land Rover with a trailer provides an uplift service that'll let the lazy among you miss out the initial climb. Call the shop for details.

JAMES DYMOND

LEARNIE
Red Rock Trails

AT A GLANCE
BEGINNERS: 2/3   **INTERMEDIATE:** 3/3   **ADVANCED:** 2/3

FACILITIES

THE TRAILS
Home	Green	0.5km
Callachy Hill Climb	Blue	1.5km
Callachy Downhill	Blue	1.3km
Muirhead Climb	Blue	1.1km
Fir Hill	Blue	0.5km
Firth View	Blue	2.2km
Fun Park	Red	1.1km
Learnie Hill	Black	3.4km

MORE INFORMATION
w: www.forestry.gov.uk

About the centre

First things first. The blue- and black-graded trails at Learnie are fantastic. For everyone else, the centre is, perhaps, a little limited. Learnie consists of individually named and graded sections of singletrack linked by forest roads – so you can create whatever sort of ride you fancy. The blue, red and green tracks are fast and swoopy – and worthwhile whatever your riding standard – while the black is a real technical challenge for good bike-handlers only. On the downside, there's a massive jump from the easier trails to the black, so progression isn't easy. The trails are also on the short side. Still, they're so good that you'll be happy to ride them time and time again.

Centre pros and cons

+ Brilliant blue-graded routes
+ Tough black route will challenge the best of riders
+ Relatively quiet
- Logging has destroyed the Fir Hill black route
- Slightly limited, though still enjoyable, for 'red-grade' riders

Directions

From Inverness, head north on the A9 for just under 8 miles to the roundabout at Tore and then turn right onto the A832, signed to Cromarty. Follow the road through the village of Rosemarkie and the trails are on your right, about 3 miles beyond the village.

Grid Ref: NH 736614   **Sat Nav:** ROSEMARKIE

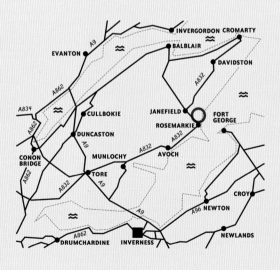

The trails

HOME	
DISTANCE: 0.5KM	**TIME:** 5 MINS
EFFORT: 1/5	**TECHNICALITY:** 2/5

A short, but enjoyable ride that barely leaves sight of the car park. The green is a downhill section of wide, well-surfaced singletrack that runs over a few easy jumps and around some gentle berms. It's fairly flat, the jumps aren't too steep or large, and everything is completely rollable. As the trail is a descent, you need to climb up to the top of it, but the climbing isn't steep and is entirely on forest roads. Beginners will love the trail and, while more experienced riders may find it a little tame, it's infinitely better than taking a fire road home.

HOWARD COTTON

CALLACHY HILL CLIMB	
DISTANCE: 1.5KM	**TIME:** 10 MINS
EFFORT: 2/5	**TECHNICALITY:** 2/5

A short and pleasant climb on narrow singletrack. The trail surface is solid, the gradient isn't steep and there are absolutely no technical difficulties, making for easy riding. You might be tackling the trail en route to the black and not particularly interested in the scenery, but the trail slips through some attractive woodland, which is always going to make a climb seem less arduous. In short, it's a trail, it climbs and it gets the job done. If you're leaving the car park and want to tackle the brilliant Callachy Downhill or the Fun Park trails, this is the way to get up to them.

CALLACHY DOWNHILL	
DISTANCE: 1.3KM	**TIME:** 10 MINS
EFFORT: 2/5	**TECHNICALITY:** 2/5

Making sweeping passes across the hillside, this is an as-fast-as-you-dare trail. Continually cornering, the lightly-bermed corners drift uphill and then dart back down again in a lovely rhythm. The odd tight corner keeps you on your toes, although it's never enough to kill your speed or steal your flow. A solid surface, a trail that's just wide enough to encourage speed, but not so wide as to kill off the corners, and a gentle gradient, mean that you can set your own pace. Brilliant!

Trails continue...

LEARNIE
continued...

MUIRHEAD CLIMB

DISTANCE: 1.1KM	TIME: 10 MINS
EFFORT: 2/5	TECHNICALITY: 2/5

Another pleasant climb – although, to be honest, it's not much of a climb, being pretty flat for most of its length. Again, a well-surfaced singletrack trail with no technical difficulties and exactly what you'd expect of a blue trail. It is worth taking if you're heading over from the car park towards the Fir Hill trails, and it's slower than the forest road alternative, but definitely more fun.

FIR HILL BLUE

DISTANCE: 500M	TIME: 5 MINS
EFFORT: 2/5	TECHNICALITY: 2/5

Yet again, the Learnie trail builders got it just right, creating another gem of a descent. As expected, the trail is solid, there's nothing in your way and you can let rip. (Within reason, of course – there might be a little old lady out walking her dog, so stay awake!) Pairs of perfect corners flow down the trail – uphill corners lift you up and drop you fast into the next smooth corner – while your speed creeps up and up. Another inspired trail.

FIRTH VIEW

DISTANCE: 2.2KM	TIME: 0.25–0.5HR
EFFORT: 2/5	TECHNICALITY: 2/5

Following on from the Fir Hill descent puts the Firth View trail at a disadvantage. Firstly, it's got a lot to live up to and, secondly, it means it starts low and ends high. Nevertheless, it's well worth riding. A pleasant climb with plenty of twists and turns brings you out onto open ground, with some fantastic views out over the Moray Firth. In fact, these are perhaps the best views of any trail centre anywhere! Some swoopy, but oh-so-short descents and more, not unpleasant, climbing bring you out to the end of the trail.

FUN PARK

DISTANCE: 1.1KM	TIME: 5 MINS
EFFORT: 1/5	TECHNICALITY: 2/5

Starting around some long, wide berms, you can carry a lot of speed into the Fun Park trail. It contains a couple of tabletops and the odd 'hump' here and there to jump. (If these are meant to be doubles, then they are MASSIVE!) It's a relatively easy trail and doesn't drop steeply, so it's easy to control your speed. This isn't a bad trail, but you need to remember that a red-graded 'Fun Park' is never going to be as big or impressive as the orange-graded set-ups found elsewhere. If you're after more corners and a greater sensation of speed, take the neighbouring blue descent. It's a lot more fun.

LEARNIE HILL

DISTANCE: 3.4KM	**TIME:** 0.5–1HR
EFFORT: 3/5	**TECHNICALITY:** 5/5

The presence of some very tricky rock gardens make Learnie Hill one of the most difficult black-graded trails in the country. Starting with an infuriating little rock-climb, the trail winds uphill via various awkward rock features. Pine-covered trails then sweep through the woods and round to a series of technical descents. Stone-slabbed, they vary in shape – some are steep, kink nastily and others follow S-bends. Fast, rooty singletrack flows between them, linking them nicely. The trail ends with a steep rocky roll back out onto forest road. One request: don't ride around the difficult bits – you're eroding the trail and missing the whole point!

Good to know

Learnie's second black-graded trail on Fir Hill has, at the time of writing, been destroyed by felling. A shame, as it was a fantastically technical route with a great descent and a testing climb. There are plans to rebuild the trail, so keep an eye on the internet for updates.

HOWARD COTTON

HOWARD COTTON

MABIE
7stanes

AT A GLANCE
BEGINNERS: 3/3 **INTERMEDIATE:** 3/3 **ADVANCED:** 3/3

FACILITIES

THE TRAILS
Big Views Loop .... Green 8km
Woodhead Loop .... Blue 10km
The Phoenix Trail .... Red 17km
Kona Dark Side .... Black 2km
Skills Park .... Orange .... N/A

NEAREST BIKE SHOP
Rik's Bike Shed (on site) – t: 01387 270 275

MORE INFORMATION
w: www.7stanes.gov.uk

Centre pros and cons

+ Good range of trails with great riding for all levels
+ The most extensive and technically difficult north shore of any trail centre
+ Youth hostel and hotel (with bar) on site
+ Easily combined with Kirroughtree, Ae or Drumlanrig for a full weekend of riding

Directions

From Dumfries, take the A710 south towards Dalbeattie. The trails are on your right after about 4 miles.

Grid Ref: NX 950707 **Sat Nav:** DG2 8HB

About the centre

As with all the 7 Stanes, Mabie offers a unique riding experience. For younger or newer riders, there are the green and blue routes – fine ways of exploring the forest. Cross-country riders will appreciate the natural-feeling singletrack of the red route, while the more daring and technically able will be challenged by the Kona Dark Side – the longest and hardest (although relatively safe) north shore trail in the UK. In addition, there's a small skills area and a Mini-X course where riders of all abilities can test and stretch their skills.

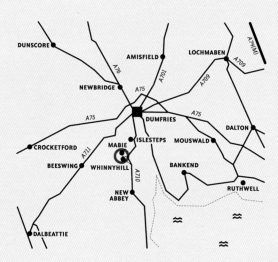

The trails

BIG VIEWS LOOP

DISTANCE: 8KM	TIME: 1–2HRS
EFFORT: 1/5	TECHNICALITY: 2/5

Unsurprisingly, the Big Views Loop passes a couple of viewpoints. Even less surprisingly, they both offer a pretty decent view out over Dumfriesshire. The remainder of the route is buried in woodland. This doesn't mean there's nothing to see, especially as you can still spot red squirrels in this part of the UK. As for the riding, it's on good, wide forest roads. There are a couple of short climbs and descents, but nothing tricky. An enjoyable way to see Mabie Forest by bike.

WOODHEAD LOOP

DISTANCE: 10KM	TIME: 1–2.5HRS
EFFORT: 2/5	TECHNICALITY: 2/5

Using forest roads to delve even deeper into the woods, the Woodhead Loop is essentially a longer version of the Big Views Loop. It's slightly longer, there's a fair bit more climbing and there's a small amount of sweeping singletrack. That said, the climbing is never too steep and the singletrack is entertaining, but relatively straightforward. A good route for fitter beginners.

THE PHOENIX TRAIL

DISTANCE: 17KM	TIME: 2–3HRS
EFFORT: 3/5	TECHNICALITY: 3/5

Fusing the natural with the manmade, The Phoenix trail is an engaging ride. Hitting singletrack early on, the trail winds up smooth tracks and easy boardwalk before shifting onto unsurfaced trails for a bit of natural fun. It gets boggy though, so it's a dry-conditions-only section. Sweeping descents and fast singletrack then lead into the heart of the forest, where rooty dirt trails wind through the trees, reminding you of a ride through your favourite local woods. A couple of rough and rocky descents bulldoze their way through the trees towards the final section of singletrack. As smooth and flowing as the best manmade trails, but on a dirt surface smattered with roots, it's a fitting finale to the ride.

Trails continue...

JAMES DYMOND

MABIE
continued...

KONA DARK SIDE	
DISTANCE: 2KM	**TIME:** 1–3HRS
EFFORT: 2/5	**TECHNICALITY:** 5/5

Undoubtedly the most technical north shore at any trail centre. Never far off the ground and with only one jump/gap at the end of the trail, the Kona Dark Side doesn't sound tricky. But when you've ridden straight off the tyre-width skinnies, dropped your back wheel off the impossibly-tight corners and stalled in the rock gardens, you'll change your mind. It's worth noting that there's a fair bit of pedalling after the first, steepest section of trail before you reach the north shore proper, but when you're there you'll be presented with the longest stretch of north shore anywhere in the UK. Brilliant.

SKILLS PARK	
DISTANCE: N/A	**TIME:** N/A
EFFORT: N/A	**TECHNICALITY:** VARIES

As well as the obligatory skills area with different, graded lines, Mabie has a Mini-X course and some dirt jumps. The dirt jumps are big, and recommended for experienced jumpers only while the Mini-X is just that – a mini 4X course. It's short, but with plenty of jumps, some of which are fairly sizeable – although all are rollable – and it is a fun course for riders of all abilities. There's also a short length of north shore running alongside the course. It's fairly straightforward, but relatively long and is high enough in places to get the old ticker going a bit faster.

HAMISH McCOOL

MORAY
Monster Trails

About the centre

Moray consists of three centres (car parks), each with its own series of trails, which can be mixed up and linked to create a ride. In the north, you have the Whiteash car park, with the Fochabers Ring and Fochabers freeride loops – good for intermediate riders. Below this is the Ordiequish car park, from where a long forest road climbs to the starts of the Dragon's Tail, Gordzilla, Gully Monster and Haggis trails. This is where to head for easy blue rides – and the awesome Gully Monster. Lastly, there's Ben Aigan, where a long forest road climb carries you up to the Ben Aigan Hammer ride, and the fast Pink Bunny and Mast Blast descents. It's here that faster riders might want to head.

Centre pros and cons

+ The Gully Monster is a fantastic trail for confident riders. Shame it's not longer!
+ Lots of short trails allow you to link sections together
+ Plenty of easier trails for less experienced riders
+ The Ben Aigan Hammer contains a 6km unbroken stretch of relatively straightforward singletrack
– A relative lack of technical singletrack trails may leave some riders wanting more

Directions

From Inverness, take the A96 south towards Aberdeen and head to Fochabers, which is about 9 miles south of Elgin. For Whiteash, turn left onto the A98 just after Fochabers – the car park is on your right after a short distance. For Ordiequish, turn right in the centre of Fochabers onto Ordiequish Road – the car park is on your left in woodland after about a mile. For Ben Aigan, follow the A96 out of Fochabers and turn right onto the A95 just before the town of Keith. Follow the road round a sharp left-hand corner at a crossroads. The car park is up a small forest road on your right 2 miles from this corner.

Whiteash: Grid Ref: NJ 358586
Ordiequish: Grid Ref: NJ 344577
Ben Aigan: Grid Ref: NJ 334493
Sat Nav: Fochabers

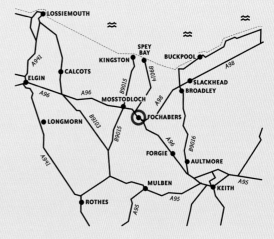

The trails

SOUP DRAGON

DISTANCE: 4KM	TIME: 0.5–1HR
EFFORT: 2/5	TECHNICALITY: 2/5

Starting with a long forest road climb up from the Ordiequish car park, the Soup Dragon (and Dragon's Tail extension) is a straightforward downhill run on smooth singletrack. Relatively wide and fairly straight with the occasional berm, it loses height gradually, meaning that, whilst a bit of pedalling will see you rocketing along, it is easy to control your speed. The trail ends at the car park, so is best ridden as a standalone loop or as a final, easy descent, unless you fancy slogging up the climb again.

GORDZILLA

DISTANCE: 5KM	TIME: 1–2HRS
EFFORT: 2/5	TECHNICALITY: 2/5

Once the long climb from the Ordiequish car park is over, Gordzilla drops downhill on a mix of trails. Using moorland doubletracks, forest roads and short sections of singletrack, the trail surface varies from hardpack to dirt to loose stone, mixing natural and manmade terrain as it does so. It's not technical and is nicely varied. The descent done, you can either drop past the campsite to link with the Whiteash centre, or climb steeply back to the top of Ordiequish. A good way for beginners to experience a few different trail surfaces.

THE HAGGIS

DISTANCE: 6KM	TIME: 0.5–1HR
EFFORT: 2/5	TECHNICALITY: 2/5

With the best flow of the blue routes on offer, the Haggis is a fun loop. It traces a high-level loop above the Ordiequish car park. Again, you've got to slog uphill to reach the trail. Once up, a fast trail, with smoothly bermed corners and small jumps here and there, flows gently downhill before the return leg climbs back to the start on singletrack and forest roads. At the southern end of the route, you can branch off the Haggis and follow cycle signs for 7km to link to the trails at Ben Aigan. At its most northerly point lie the Soup Dragon, Gully Monster and Gordzilla trails. The Haggis is both a good way of linking centres and an enjoyable extension to one of the other rides.

FOCHABERS RING

DISTANCE: 8KM	TIME: 1–2HRS
EFFORT: 3/5	TECHNICALITY: 3/5

With a real mix of trails, the Fochabers Ring is a solid addition to the Moray trails. The trail warms up along some flat forest double track before swinging sharply uphill for a massive climb on forest roads. It's steep in places, and just before the top it narrows and becomes rockier. Passing over the top on wide trails, the trail ducks through some gloomy woods on tight singletrack before heading out onto a pleasant cruise across open land. From here, the trail gradually begins to twist and turn, and soon rattles down a loose gully onto a fantastic section of wooded trail that wriggles through the trees and over roots to the car park. Enjoyed it? Head over to the Gully Monster next.

Trails continue...

FOCHABERS FREERIDE

DISTANCE: 0.75KM	TIME: N/A
EFFORT: 1/5	TECHNICALITY: 4/5

Dropping from the top of Fochabers Ring, the freeride trail has two distinct halves. Up top is a short section of wide north shore. It's high in places, but not particularly long and with no drops or skinny sections. Probably not worth visiting the centre just for this… The second half is, essentially a short and easy downhill run. It's well-surfaced and wide, but fairly fast as a result. The usual array of jumps and berms is used to good effect to create an enjoyable trail that spits you out halfway down the Fochabers Ring descent.

BEN AIGAN HAMMER

DISTANCE: 8KM	TIME: 1–2HRS
EFFORT: 3/5	TECHNICALITY: 2/5

The Hammer consists of an unbroken singletrack lap around the summit of Ben Aigan. It's fairly rocky, though never technical, and undulates throughout its length. It's pleasant riding – absorbing, if not demanding – and there are some great views along the way. There is a short section of boardwalk with an optional drop and some avoidable jumps near the end of the trail to provide technical interest, but to be honest, they seem slightly out of character with the rest of the trail. As is standard with the Moray trails, there's a big forest road climb to reach the singletrack loop, and you can link the trail with either the Pink Bunny or Mast Blast descents on your return to the car park.

PINK BUNNY TRAIL

DISTANCE: 1KM	TIME: 5 MINS
EFFORT: 2/5	TECHNICALITY: 3/5

By far the most technical trail at Ben Aigan, the Pink Bunny Trail kicks off across open moorland with some long berms and small tabletop jumps. It then moves swiftly into the woods where the going becomes tight, narrower, steeper and generally more interesting. It's twisty in places, with a great flow, and crosses contrived rock gardens and small drops here and there. Leaving the woods again, the trail picks up speed with some bigger berms and some sizeable doubles. Fast drops lead down to the forest road and the return to the car park. A good trail.

DAVID SMITH

MAST BLAST

DISTANCE: 1KM	TIME: 5 MINS
EFFORT: 1/5	TECHNICALITY: 3/5

Easier than the Pink Bunny and infinitely more enjoyable than
the forest road alternative, the Mast Blast is a good way to end
a lap of the Ben Aigan Hammer. With a good surface, it's a fast
trail and the bermed corners hold speed well. Apart from a few
rollable jumps, there are no sharp corners or technical sections
to catch you out, and the trail follows a shallow gradient – so
speeds are easily controllable. Hit it hard for some real fun,
or take it easy for an enjoyable cruise.

GULLY MONSTER

DISTANCE: 2KM	TIME: 0.25HR
EFFORT: 2/5	TECHNICALITY: 3/5

Gully Monster? More like a ravine! (The name wouldn't sound
as good though.) Beginning with tight, natural singletrack
through the trees, the Gully Monster starts off innocently
enough. Suddenly diving down towards the river, the trail
nips around some steep switchbacks to cling precipitously to
the side of a steep slope as the valley bottom drops away
beneath it. A narrow trail then traverses high above the river,
inching around tight, blind corners and over off-camber slopes.
Shy away from the drop and you risk catching a pedal on the
steep bank to your right. Keep clear of the bank and the drop
beckons! An outstanding trail.

Good to know

The three centres can be linked to create a monster ride.
The Ben Aigan and Ordiequish trails can be linked via a half-
hour ride on wide cycle tracks. You can then reach the
Whiteash trails by dropping down from Gordzilla towards the
campsite and then riding along the main road, or by riding
between the car parks via Fochabers town centre.

DAVID SMITH

MULL OF KINTYRE
Wee Toon Trails

About the centre

The 'Wee Toon Trails' in Beinn Ghuilean Forest beside
Campbeltown on the Mull of Kintyre were opened in May 2007.
Designed as multi-purpose trails intended to suit mountain
bikers and walkers, the trails were funded by local groups.
They are not particularly long or technical, but make a nice
addition to the many outdoor activities already on offer in the
area. Sitting in the woods above Campbeltown, the trails are
reached by a twenty-minute ride from the town itself.

Centre pros and cons

+ Pleasant trails in a picturesque part of Scotland
+ Starting at the leisure centre means a full range of facilities
− Very short trails – probably not worth the two-hour plus
  round trip
− Riding up from the town adds twenty minutes of tarmac
  climbing to the ride

Directions

Head down the Mull of Kintyre to Campbeltown. Once there,
head to the Quays on the seafront and turn left. The Aqualibrium
will be straight in front of you. Pick up a map from The
Aqualibriumto find the start of the trails.

Grid Ref: NR 720206   **Sat Nav:** PA28 6EG

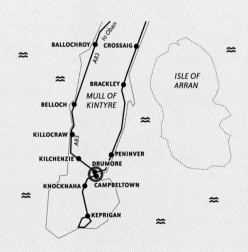

The trails

BLUE TRAIL	
DISTANCE: 2.7KM	**TIME:** 20 MINS
EFFORT: 2/5	**TECHNICALITY:** 2/5

The blue trail begins with a twenty-minute ride uphill from
the town centre. It's steep in places and young children might
not appreciate it. Once you're on the trail though, it's pretty
good fun. Relatively narrow, with some interesting corners
and dips to swoop in and out of, the trail begins with a fun,
flowing descent. There are some open views out over
Campbeltown, which adds to the trail's appeal. After a couple
of bermed corners, the trail swings back on itself for a long,
gentle climb back up to the trailhead.

RED TRAIL	
DISTANCE: 2KM	**TIME:** 15 MINS
EFFORT: 3/5	**TECHNICALITY:** 2/5

The red is an add-on to the blue route, swinging off early on
and rejoining a short distance further on, adding a climb and
a descent as it does so. The trail is entirely singletrack and is
relatively wide and well-surfaced. There's nothing particularly
technical about it and, to be honest, it's not quite as much fun
as the blue. Having said that, the climb is pleasant, twisting
uphill around hairpins and through pleasant surroundings.
The descent, meanwhile, is slightly trickier, with a couple of
berms to keep you on your toes.

Good to know
Pick up a map from The Aqualibrium to find the start of the trails.

JOHN COEFIELD

JOHN COEFIELD

NEWCASTLETON
7stanes

About the centre

Newcastleton is the Stane to head for if you're after easy singletrack riding. There's a green-graded skills area and a forest road route to warm up on before tackling the blue-graded singletrack descent of the Caddrouns route. After that, there are 10.5km of gentle, flowing singletrack on Newcastleton's red route – perfect for the more adventurous. None of the riding is technically difficult and there are no major climbs, meaning that the routes are fairly easy for their grades. This isn't to say that they're not enjoyable – well-surfaced, fast singletrack always is – meaning that this is a perfect centre for those looking for an easy, but fun, day out.

Centre pros and cons

+ A wide choice of blue-graded trails and an easy red make Newcastleton a good centre for intermediate riders
+ A skills area for beginners and north shore for more advanced riders
− Limited technical riding but Kielder is only a short drive away (see page 58)

Directions

From Carlisle, follow the A7 north towards Hawick. After about 13 miles (just before Canonbie), turn right onto the B6357 and follow this to Newcastleton village. Just before entering the village, turn right, crossing a bridge onto a minor road and follow this up the hill. The car park is on your right at the top.

Grid Ref: NY 502874   **Sat Nav:** TD9 0TD

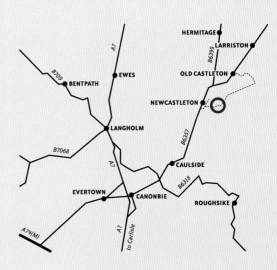

The trails

CADDROUNS	
DISTANCE: 7KM	**TIME:** 1–2HRS
EFFORT: 2/5	**TECHNICALITY:** 2/5

LINNS	
DISTANCE: 8KM	**TIME:** 1–2HRS
EFFORT: 2/5	**TECHNICALITY:** 1/5

Newcastleton has two contrasting blue routes for intermediate riders – the forest road Linns loop and the singletrack Caddrouns. The Linns is the longer of the two and climbs up into the forest on good tracks. There are no real views, but you're riding alongside rivers and through large clearings, so the surroundings are pleasant. A nice, mellow ride. The Caddrouns loop uses forest road to gain height, but then winds back down the hill on wide, smooth singletrack. With plenty of corners, some gentle berms and not much pedalling, it's as fast as you want to make it and good fun.

RED	
DISTANCE: 16KM	**TIME:** 1.5–3HRS
EFFORT: 3/5	**TECHNICALITY:** 3/5

Kicking off with a snaking descent that winds around switchbacks and between trees, Newcastleton's red route is down at the easier end of the grade. It's not technical, but that's not to say it isn't fun. There are no rock gardens, root-infested trails or jumps to contend with, but the sinuous singletrack is great to ride. It's pleasant, rather than adrenaline-fuelled, riding and that makes it a good choice for an easier day out. And of course, smooth singletrack with flowing corners has never lent itself to being ridden flat out, or has it…?

Other riding

Newcastleton has a green graded skills area. Easier than the skills areas at the other 7 Stanes, it contains some low boardwalk, a couple of berms and some rollable jumps. Beside this is a reasonably extensive set of north shore trails. There are a few different lines, including some skinny(ish) sections. It's nowhere near as hard as Mabie, but trickier than Glentree's Ewok Village (and mildly terrifying if you're clipped in ready for the Red route). It's not worth travelling to Newcastleton just for the north shore, but if you're there and aren't averse to balancing along bits of wood, it's a decent addition to the centre.

DOUG INGLIS

PITFICHIE

About the centre

Sending you out into what feels like the middle of nowhere, Pitfichie has a nice, remote feel to it. There's a long forest road route, offering a pleasant easy ride with good views and a couple of downhill runs that are as fast and sketchy as big-bike enthusiasts could want. Technical cross-country is catered for by the red route, which contains two contrasting sections of riding – one natural and one manmade. It's on the short side and, with only two, albeit long, sections of singletrack, it won't fill a whole day, but is good fun nonetheless.

Centre pros and cons

+ Fantastic 'wilderness' feel
+ Technical downhill runs
+ Nice mix of manmade and natural singletrack on the red XC route
+ Enjoyable easier route with some pleasant views
− The red route is on the short side

Directions

From Aberdeen, take the A96 north towards Inverness. After 11 miles, turn right at the roundabout onto the B994 and then, following signs for Kemnay at the roundabouts, stay on the B994 westbound. Continue onto the B993 as the two roads merge and follow this to Monymusk village. Go through the village and turn right after 2 miles. The car park is on your left after about half a mile.

Grid Ref: NJ 656132   **Sat Nav:** MONYMUSK

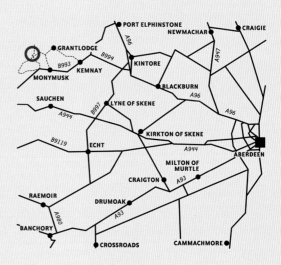

The trails

WHITE ROUTE

DISTANCE: 15KM	TIME: 1–3HRS
EFFORT: 3/5	TECHNICALITY: 2/5

This is a technically easy ride of a decent length, although it requires a bit of fitness, and it rewards riders with great views. Sound good? Pitfichie provides you with a pleasant couple of hours riding. Following mainly fire roads, but throwing in some forest doubletrack to keep things interesting, the White Route circles around Cairn William and Pitfichie Hill. Although it doesn't climb too high, the immediate countryside is a little lower than the trail, so there are some good views out over Aberdeenshire. All in all, a fine easy route.

RED

DISTANCE: 7KM	TIME: 1–2HRS
EFFORT: 3/5	TECHNICALITY: 4/5

Branching off the White Route, Pitfichie's red is a series of trails that form a 'T'. At the bottom is a two-way section of technical, natural riding. It begins with a stiff climb into the woods before moving out of the trees for a steep and technical rocky moorland climb. A dab-free ascent here would be something special. More satisfyingly rocky trails lead to a fire road and the only one-way section of singletrack on the route. Climbing across moorland, a smooth trail leads between rock slabs. Once up, a fast, bermed descent criss-crosses the slope, getting twistier as it drops. This singletrack ends on a ridge. On either side is a very fast forest road descent (the top section of the 'T') while straight ahead lay the downhill runs. Take your pick.

DOWNHILL

DISTANCE: 1.2KM	TIME: N/A
EFFORT: N/A	TECHNICALITY: 4/5

Pitfichie's downhill runs are rocky, rooty and natural. The top, open section is relatively straightforward – hit the rocks hard and fast and hang on. Entering the trees, the trail widens and multiple line choices appear through the trees. Pick one and hang on over the bumps and rocks. Don't get caught out by the off-camber roots and hit the drops at the bottom as fast as you like. Good technical riding.

HOWARD COTTON

STRATHPEFFER

About the centre

If you like tight, technical riding, visit Contin Forest near Strathpeffer. It's full of the stuff. Not a trail centre as such, Contin is simply a forest containing some great natural riding, some of which has been waymarked by Square Wheels, the local bike shop. They've also mapped other routes of varying difficulty through the forest, including the course of the Strathpuffer 24 hr Race. It's held in the middle of the Scottish winter making other endurance events seem like a ride to the chip shop and back! The waymarked riding is best-suited to technically able riders, although there's plenty of good stuff in the area, no matter what your level.

Centre pros and cons

+ Fantastic tight, natural and technical singletrack
+ ...and there's loads of it – go and explore
+ Lovely forest setting
- Hard to find the start of the trails – pick up a map from Square Wheels in Strathpeffer
- Can get muddy in the winter
- Nothing marked for beginners, although there are suitable trails on the Square Wheels map

Directions

From Inverness, follow the A9 north for 7 miles to the Tore roundabout. Turn left onto the A835 and follow this to Contin. Go through the village and, on a sharp left-hand bend just after leaving the majority of the houses, turn right into the woods. Follow the track to the car park.

Grid Ref: NH 452571   **Sat Nav:** CONTIN

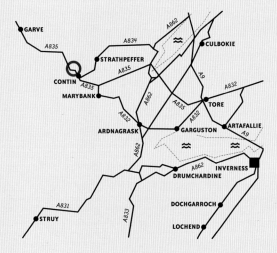

The trails

RED TRAIL

DISTANCE: 16KM	TIME: 1–2HRS
EFFORT: 3/5	TECHNICALITY: 4/5

Once you've found the start of the trail, you're straight onto natural singletrack through loamy forest. Weaving about, the trail cuts around tight corners, taking narrow lines between trees. It's rooty in places, making line choice critical, especially when you're trying to duck through a tight gap and avoid a root at the same time! Plenty of short, sharp climbs and descents and the odd granite slab here and there add to the fun. The route can get boggy in the winter, and although there's the odd plank or rock bridge keeping you out of the worst of it, the trail is at its best in the summer, or when frozen solid. A great trail for those who like technical forest singletrack.

Good to know

- The easiest place to park for the red route is in the Torrachilty Forest Car Park just outside Contin. To find the start of the trail, ride back towards the road and take the first forest road on the left. Climb to the top and turn right, following signs right to Strathpeffer. You'll soon pick up the red arrows.
- At the end of the trail you'll pop out on to a fire road. Turn left and follow this to the start of the route. Either ride another lap, follow the fire road home or make up a return route; perhaps by taking the singletrack descent on your right.
- You will need a map – get one from Square Wheels in Strathpeffer.

GARY WILLIAMSON

TOP 10:
Flowing Singletrack

Technically straightforward and easy to ride, these are smooth and sweeping trails – incredible fun to ride fast, it's impossible not to enjoy them.

1   Kirroughtree's Twister
Will there ever be a manmade trail that flows better than this?

2   Cwmcarn's Twrch Trail
Technical(ish) going up, smooth, fast and oh-so-much-fun on the way back down.

3   Glentress's red and blue trails
It may be crowded and the trails are a bit battered yet people keep heading there to ride. Must be something in the water…

4   Swinley Forest
Large forest + stacks of singletrack = lots of fun.

5   Penmachno (both loops)
Classic, old-skool (with a 'k') – call it what you like, these are XC trails at their best.

6   Cannock Chase's Follow the Dog
The mud's long gone, but the fast, twisty trails remain.

7   Thetford's red
The faster you ride, the better it gets.

8   Surrey Hills
Three hills, lots of trees, plenty of singletrack.

9   Afan Argoed (all of 'em)
Technical in places, but never too hard and brilliant fun to ride fast.

10 Golspie's red
Smooth climbing, fast berms and crafted drops – perfect flow (just don't venture onto the black).

SECTION 3
WALES

AFAN ARGOED

AT A GLANCE

BEGINNERS: 1/3   **INTERMEDIATE:** 3/3   **EXPERT:** 3/3

FACILITIES

(Both centres)

THE TRAILS

Penyhdd	Red	17km
The Wall	Red	23km
White's Level	Red	15km
Skyline	Black	46km

NEAREST BIKE SHOP

Skyline Cycles, Glyncorrwg – t: 01639 850 011
Skyline Cycles, Afan Visitor Centre – t: 01639 851 100

MORE INFORMATION

www.mbwales.com
Afan Forest Park Visitor Centre – t: 01639 850 564
Glyncorrwg Mountain Bike Centre – t: 01639 851 900

About the centre

Afan Argoed consists of two centres. The older of the two, by the Afan visitor centre, contains the Penhydd and The Wall trails. The second, newer centre is just up the road at Glyncorrwyg and is home to the White's Level and Skyline trails. Both centres have bike shops, cafés and campsites (the Drop Off Café at Glyncorrwg is fantastic). It's possible to ride between the two along the valley or across the hilltops (a waymarked White's Level—The Wall route is planned). For the most part, the riding is rough, flowing singletrack – 'traditional' XC trail centre riding – suitable for pretty much everyone bar complete beginners. Quick riders will appreciate the fast trails while those with less experience should find the singletrack challenging, but still a lot of fun.

Centre pros and cons

+ Fast, rough and flowing singletrack
+ Enough riding to fill a weekend, and enough facilities to stay on site
+ The Drop Off café at Glyncorrwg serves good, cheap food, has an alcohol licence and opens late. The bike shop there is pretty big and the campsite is decent.
− Some of the routes contain a bit too much fire road
− No trails for complete beginners

Directions

Turn off the M4 at J40 and head north under the motorway. Turn left at the mini-roundabout onto the A4107, following signs to Afan Forest Park. The Afan car park is on your right after about 5 miles. For Glyncorrwg, continue 3 miles to Cymmer and turn left following signs for Glyncorrwg. The centre is on your left, just before the village.

Afan
Grid Ref: SS 821951   **Sat Nav:** SA13 3HG
Glyncorrwg
Grid Ref: SS 872984   **Sat Nav:** SA13 3EA

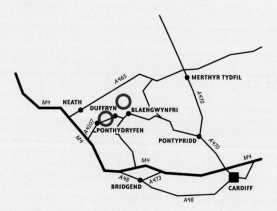

The trails

PENYHDD

DISTANCE: 17KM	TIME: 1.5–3HRS
EFFORT: 3/5	TECHNICALITY: 3/5

This was the first trail opened at Afan, and it's a classic. In true 'old school' style, it uses forest roads to gain height before letting rip along some pretty unforgettable sections of singletrack. This singletrack is good, and it's varied. There's the Hidden Valley, dropping fast through the trees on worryingly narrow, rooty dirt track. Further on is the Sidewinder, a series of loose, stony switchbacks and off-the-brakes corners that cross open ground before nipping into the woods for the flowing bends of Dead Sheep Gully. A good 'little' trail, it's the easiest and least technical here, but no less enjoyable for it.

THE WALL

DISTANCE: 24KM	TIME: 1–2.5HRS
EFFORT: 3/5	TECHNICALITY: 3/5

The Wall is, as they say, a ride of two halves. The first, despite containing some decent singletrack, is dominated by forest roads (you might wonder, at points, if you've missed a turning…). The second, and better, half consists almost entirely of superb singletrack and will have you contemplating a second lap. The singletrack is long, rough and very, very fast. Less-experienced riders will find the riding challenging but fun, whereas faster riders can hit the rocks, switchbacks and compressions flat out and have a blast. This is 'traditional' trail centre singletrack at its very best.

WHITE'S LEVEL

DISTANCE: 15KM	TIME: 2–3HRS
EFFORT: 3/5	TECHNICALITY: 3/5

The White's Level hits singletrack just outside the car park, and stays on it for the next 15km. The first half hour or so is climbing. Luckily it's on a trail with enough technical interest to stop you from realising you're going uphill. At the top, there's an optional black-graded descent around big, rough berms (it returns to the same point) before the trail shoots off along a long, twisting run. The new Energy section then throws in a couple of jumps and some tight, tight singletrack before things really start to flow around the corners of Goodwood. A final technical descent plummets at warp speed over rocks and drops to provide a thrilling finish to this brilliant route.

Trails continue…

TIM RUSSON

AFAN ARGOED
continued...

SKYLINE

DISTANCE: 46KM	**TIME:** 4–7HRS
EFFORT: 5/5	**TECHNICALITY:** 3/5

If you're at Afan and want a full day's riding, you can either link up a couple of the shorter trails or head out along the Skyline. It's a long, hard ride, but with some awesome sections of singletrack that more than compensate you for the effort put in. Unfortunately, there's a fair amount (ok, a lot) of forest road on the Skyline, which puts many people off tackling it. If you feel this way, you can always take one of the two shortcuts (at roughly one-third and two-thirds distance) on the route. No matter whether you wimp out or make it all the way round, you'll always get to ride the final two sections of singletrack (around 10km of narrow, twisty descending!), which are brilliant.

Good to know

- There are fast tracks between the two centres along the bottom of the valley and also a higher link between the tops of the White's Level and Wall Trails. This latter option will soon become a waymarked route ('W2' – graded Black).
- If you've heard of the 'July' route but can't find it, it's the name given to the loop created by taking the first shortcut on the Skyline.
- If you're staying over, both centres have good campsites, although, in winter, only Glyncorrwg is open. The excellent Drop Off café, with its good, cheap food, late opening hours and alcohol licence puts in a convincing argument for staying at Glyncorrwg.

TIM RUSSON

BRECHFA

About the centre

Brechfa is a huge forest to the west of the Brecon Beacons. As you might expect, given the location, it's an attractive region with some great natural riding. Designed by downhill rider Rowan Sorrell, the idea behind the manmade trails was to add something completely different to the area. With that in mind, the red-graded Gorlech Trail was built with a fast and jumpy 'big BMX track through the woods' style. It was followed by green and blue graded routes of a similar, although obviously easier, nature (the green route is one of the best in the UK). Completing Brechfa's set of routes is the black-graded Raven Trail. More natural and technical, it means that Brechfa really does have a trail for everyone.

Centre pros and cons

+ Great for those who want to pump and jump their way around the trails
+ Fantastic 'BMX-style' descents
+ Very much all-weather routes – well-surfaced and sheltered
+ The green route is a fantastic and fun introduction to mountain biking
+ Picnic benches and shelters are a nice touch
– Signage could be better in places

Directions

From Carmarthen, head east on the A40 towards Llandeilo. Turn left (north) onto the B4310 at Nantgaredig and follow this up through Brechfa. Parking for the green, blue and black trails is on your left between Brechfa and Nant-y-ffin. For the Gorlech Trail, continue along the B4310 to Abergorlech. The car park is again on your left in the middle of the village.

Grid Ref: SN 545315   **Sat Nav:** BRECHFA

Abergorlech   **Grid Ref:** SN 585340

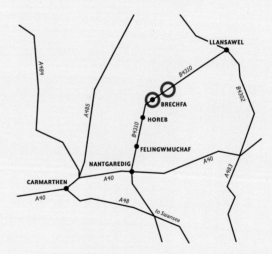

The trails

DERWEN TRAIL

DISTANCE: 9KM	TIME: 1–2HRS
EFFORT: 2/5	TECHNICALITY: 2/5

If you're going to build a green mountain bike trail for beginners, this is how you should do it. A proper mountain bike ride, the Derwen Trail sweeps through the forest on well-surfaced, wide singletrack. Weaving and swooping between the trees, the trail is easy enough for children, but enough fun for experienced riders. Chuck in some attractive surroundings and a couple of picnic benches and you have a real gem of a route. Know someone who wants a gentle introduction to mountain biking? This is where you should bring them.

DERWEN TRAIL EXTENSION

DISTANCE: 5KM	TIME: 0.75–1HR
EFFORT: 3/5	TECHNICALITY: 2/5

An extension of the green route, the blue breaks away from that trail at the halfway point, adding an extra climb and descent. The riding surface is good, the climb isn't too hard and the singletrack is fairly wide. It is, however, a definite step up in difficulty from the green. There are more corners and, as the trail is raised slightly above the forest floor, the penalty for creeping off-line is more severe. The descent is as fast as you want it to be, with multiple lines, berms and a couple of (surprisingly big) tabletop jumps near the end. A fun trail for those wanting to push themselves a bit harder.

GORLECH TRAIL

DISTANCE: 22KM	TIME: 1.5–3HRS
EFFORT: 3/5	TECHNICALITY: 3/5

It's the descents that you'll remember after riding this route. To reach them, though, you'll have to ride uphill, and the route contains a fair bit of forest road climbing. Luckily, it also features some good singletrack climbs where the gradient and corners have been crafted to make you feel as though you are being pulled uphill. On the way down, the trail becomes a roller coaster. Big berms, pumping compressions and lofting jumps create a trail that's all rollable, but that gets better and better the faster you push. And the descent with the biggest berms, the steepest jumps and the highest speeds is right where it should be – at the very end, making sure you finish the trail with a bang.

RAVEN TRAIL

DISTANCE: 18KM	TIME: 1–2HRS
EFFORT: 3/5	TECHNICALITY: 4/5

The Raven Trail mixes the big-bermed, jumpy style of riding found on the other routes at Brechfa with predominantly natural singletrack. The singletrack is tight in places and fast in others (yet always fun), while the majority of the descents arc around big berms and jumps. You won't get the most out of them on your first time down, but they get better and better with familiarity. There's a lot of forest road climbing on the route and the riding isn't particularly technical for a black-graded trail (if anything, the final descent on the red trail – which can be linked from the black for a mammoth day out – is harder!) but it's a good all-round ride that's a fine test of your fitness, singletrack riding and jumping skills.

CLI-MACHX

AT A GLANCE
BEGINNERS: 0/3   **INTERMEDIATE:** 3/3   **ADVANCED:** 2/3

FACILITIES

THE TRAIL
Cli-machx . . . . Red 15km

NEAREST BIKE SHOP
The Holey Trail, Machynlleth – **t:** 01654 700 411

MORE INFORMATION
w: www.dyfimountainbiking.org.uk   **w:** www.mbwales.com

Centre pros and cons
+ Finishes on the longest singletrack descent in Wales
+ Good quality singletrack of various styles
+ Technical climbs are a nice touch on a manmade trail
+ Ideally located close to lots more great riding
− No facilities but Machynlleth is close by

Directions
Head north from Machynlleth on the A487 towards Dolgellau and turn right to Ceinws (following the little bunny-hopping cyclist signs). Cross the river and follow signs to the left and uphill.

Grid Ref: SH 759063   **Sat Nav:** MACHYNLLETH

About the centre
The cunningly-named Cli-machx trail is a purpose-built singletrack trail just outside Machynlleth that builds and builds to a dramatic finale. Once the capital of Wales, Machynlleth is now a good base for visiting mountain bikers, with a range of shops, eateries and, most importantly, riding. Along with the Cli-machx, there are three waymarked Mach routes *(see page 192)* and the centres of Coed y Brenin and Nant yr Arian lie a short way to the north and south respectively. That's without even mentioning the natural riding or the array of events held in the area throughout the year!

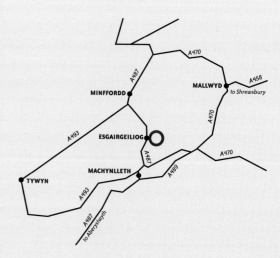

The trail

CLI-MACHX

DISTANCE: 15KM	**TIME:** 1–2HRS
EFFORT: 3/5	**TECHNICALITY:** 4/5

It's the final downhill of the Cli-machx trail that people talk about. It's one of the longest singletrack descents in the UK. Deep in the forest, it's dark, rocky and highly technical at the top and curves around a series of large berms at the bottom. Not a descent to be taken lightly, it's pretty hard to ride fast and smoothly – but it feels great when you do. You can reach it directly from the first climb, or miss it out altogether, but why would you want to do either? The remainder of the trail features good singletrack. It's fairly swoopy with the odd tricky section and contains a couple of rocky, technical climbs – nice to see at a trail centre.

JAMES DYMOND

JAMES DYMOND

COED LLANDEGLA

About the centre

Coed Llandegla brings a completely different style of riding to north Wales. Opened in late 2005, it gives a new meaning to the 'something for everyone' cliché, with green and blue routes for beginners, a reasonable red route for intermediate riders and its infamous black route for those wanting to go fast. Generally speaking, the centre does away with technical rocky sections and tight corners, choosing instead to roll out smooth trails, berms and jumps for you to hit at warp speed. Whichever trail you chose, there's a good bike shop and a fantastic café waiting at the end.

Centre pros and cons

+ A good range of routes makes this a centre for all levels of riding ability
+ The unique black route – smooth and full of jumps and berms, it's as fast as you want it to be!
+ The hard-packed surface of most of the trails holds up well in all weather, although there are some muddy sections
+ Great café and decent bike shop
− Long and relatively dull climb to start the blue, red and black routes
− No natural or technical (in a traditional sense) trails

Directions

From Wrexham, take the A525 signed towards Ruthin. Coed Llandegla is up a minor road on your left about 8 miles from the centre of Wrexham.

Grid Ref: SJ 227520   **Sat Nav:** LL11 3AA

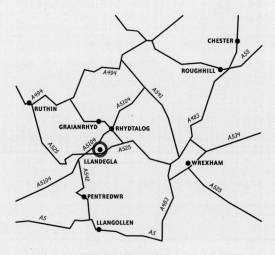

The trails

GREEN	
DISTANCE: 5KM	**TIME:** 0.5–1HR
EFFORT: 2/5	**TECHNICALITY:** 1/5

A lake at the top and a decent café at the bottom – a winning combination for a family cycle ride if ever there was one! Following wide tracks, the route climbs, steeply in places, up to the reservoir. Once up top, there are picnic benches and good views out over the Clwydian hills. The lap of the reservoir is partly on a grassy surface and can get soggy after rain, but it's not long, so don't worry too much. A fun, swoopy descent on wide tracks (you can always take one of the harder blue or red descents if you want a challenge) brings you to within a few metres of a great range of cakes in the café.

BLUE	
DISTANCE: 12 KM	**TIME:** 1–2HRS
EFFORT: 3/5	**TECHNICALITY:** 2/5

As it should be, Llandegla's blue-graded route is an ideal next step up from the green. After a seemingly never-ending climb (although, to be fair, it's on a good surface and through a pleasant forest), the blue route swings downhill. The surface is always good, the trails are wide and the corners are fun. Although the top of the route is shared with the red and contains a few enjoyable berms, the route is far from technical. Great for fitter families and inexperienced riders wanting a gentle ride.

Trails continue…

DAN BARHAM

COED LLANDEGLA
continued...

RED

DISTANCE: 18KM	TIME: 1.5–3HRS
EFFORT: 3/5	TECHNICALITY: 3/5

BLACK

DISTANCE: 21KM	TIME: 1.5–3HRS
EFFORT: 4/5	TECHNICALITY: 3/5

Beginning with a long, exciting climb (that's sarcasm, by the way – the initial climb drags on a bit!), the route 'proper' kicks off with a promising descent around berms and over some big jumps. From there, rough singletrack cuts up and down through the forest. It's pretty standard red-grade singletrack – enjoyable but not too technical, although it does gets muddy, (but thankfully not sticky), in the wet. From there on, a quick descent, a fair amount of climbing and a strange, rattley 'log boardwalk' lead to the final descent to the café.

Don't come to Llandegla expecting subtle, natural singletrack. With a smooth, hard surface, berms around every corner and jumps on every straight, this is the route people come to ride at Llandegla. Cutting off the red route for a 6km BMX-track-through-the-woods style detour, the black is eye-wateringly fast. The berms are perfectly shaped, the jumps are rollable but easy to clear and the gently descending singletrack goes on forever. Don't be put off trying it – it's never steep, so you can control your speed easily. It's not all swooping descents though – this is an XC trail and so you've got to repay gravity for the fun you've had with some big climbs. A fun route.

© MBR (MOUNTAIN BIKE RIDER) MAGAZINE

COED TRALLWM

Centre pros and cons

+ Enjoyable, natural-feeling singletrack
+ Technically straightforward, steep trails that are good fun
+ Good facilities
− Nothing for complete beginners

Directions

From Llandovery, at the north west corner of the Brecon Beacons, take the A40 west, and then, just on leaving the town, turn right onto the A483, heading north towards Builth Wells. Stay on the A483 for 15 miles to Beulah and then turn left onto a minor road, signed towards Abergwesyn. The centre is another 4 miles along this road.

Grid Ref: SN 882543   **Sat Nav:** LD5 4TS

About the centre

Situated close to Llanwrtyd Wells, home to unusual sporting events like the World Bog Snorkelling Championships and the Man v Horse v Bike Race, Coed Trallwm is a small biking centre offering three good, if short, singletrack trails. Also boasting a very friendly log-cabin café (homemade cakes!), several self-catering cottages and a decent range of facilities, the centre is within driving distance of the larger centres of Afan and Brechfa, and of the Brecon Beacons. There are no trails for complete beginners, but for intermediate and above riders, all three trails offer some good singletrack. It currently costs £2 to ride at Coed Trallwm.

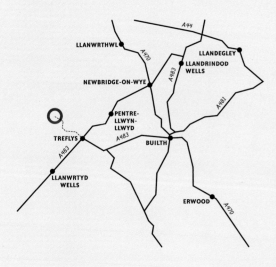

The trails

BLUE	
DISTANCE: 4KM	**TIME:** 0.5–1HR
EFFORT: 2/5	**TECHNICALITY:** 3/5

BLACK	
DISTANCE: 6KM	**TIME:** 0.5–1HR
EFFORT: 3/5	**TECHNICALITY:** 3/5

All three trails at Coed Trallwm share the same start – well-surfaced, fast singletrack with an avoidable stream crossing to begin with. The blue route then heads up a long forest road before the trail narrows and heads into the woods. It starts off fast, but things tighten up and narrow as you drop down towards a river. The trail here can get muddy in winter, which makes a few of the corners a bit spicy, but is otherwise good, fast fun. The trail then twists across some rocky open ground before returning to the cover of the trees for a sweeping run back to the start. A good trail.

The black follows the blue, but misses out the final descent of that route, continuing up a big forest track climb. The track eventually narrows to singletrack and follows the edge of the wood to the high point of the route, from where there are some great views and a real wilderness feel. The descent drops straight down some very steep and straight trails, which means you rapidly pick up speed and need to be good with the brakes if you want to make the tight corners – especially in the wet! Dropping into the woods, the trail swings around a few tight corners and then hits a series of big berms before spitting you out into the car park.

RED	
DISTANCE: 5KM	**TIME:** 0.75–1.5HRS
EFFORT: 3/5	**TECHNICALITY:** 2/5

After the shared start, the red trail crosses the road and heads away from the centre on a big forest road climb. There's a fair bit of height gain, which means a big descent. The following singletrack, which makes a series of straight passes across the slope, is slightly disappointing when compared with the blue, as it lacks corners. Still, it's fast, rough and leads into a twistier section of trail which is much more interesting. This is followed by the obligatory trail centre boardwalk section and then a less conventional river crossing. It's deep and has a fiddly exit – you're going to get wet feet!

COED Y BRENIN

Centre pros and cons

+ The most trails of any trail centre in the UK
+ Great for technical XC riding
+ There's a nice variety of singletrack – fast and smooth, slow and technical
+ Good facilities
− Can get busy and congested
− Nothing for jumpers or freeriders

Directions

From Dolgellau, head north on the A470, towards Betws-y-Coed and Porthmadog. Go straight ahead at the roundabout and the centre is signposted on your right after about 5 miles.

Grid ref: SH 720270   **Sat Nav:** LL40 2HY

About the centre

When the first trail at Coed y Brenin, the Red Bull, was opened in 1997, the first dedicated trail centre in the world was created. It was a phenomenal success and paved the way for the 60+ centres now dotted around the UK – quite an achievement. Without the efforts of a number of people, including Dafydd Davis, Sian and Dafydd Roberts and Patrick Adams, and without the backing of Forest Enterprise, the British mountain biking scene today would be very different. Now, Coed y Brenin is the largest trail centre in Britain, with six trails, five of which are technical XC trails graded red or above.

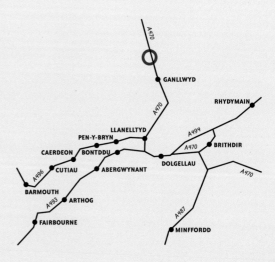

The trails

YR AFON' TRAIL

DISTANCE: 7/11KM	TIME: 1–3HRS
EFFORT: 2/5	TECHNICAL: 1/5

A nice family trail, mainly on very good surfaces. The route leaves the centre on a section of built trail (still around 2m wide), then follows roads and tracks to trace a picturesque loop alongside the River Mawddach. You'll pass the abandoned gold mines of Gwynfynedd and plenty of spots from which to watch the river, with its rapids and rocky sections. A pleasant ride, suitable for children and for those after an easy ride.

TEMTIWR TRAIL

DISTANCE: 9KM	TIME: 0.5–1HR
EFFORT: 2/5	TECHNICALITY: 2/5

The Temtiwr is a quick-hit Coed y Brenin 'teaser'. Mixing singletrack sections from the Dragon's Back and MBR routes, it might be short, but it's pretty technical and climbs a big hill. Leaving the visitor centre, the trail nips out along the rocky Badger and then the Pinderosa singletracks. They look technical, but the intimidating rock slabs have been carefully positioned to create a fast, flowing ride. Next up are the smooth berms of Dream Time and a long forest road drag up to the start of the final descent. Far more technical than the earlier singletrack, this is a fast, rough and rocky blast. A short, but varied and entertaining trail.

MBR TRAIL

DISTANCE: 18.4KM	TIME: 1.5–3HRS
EFFORT: 3/5	TECHNICALITY: 3/5

The MBR has long been a staple of Coed y Brenin and, despite the passing of thousands of wheels and violent storms sweeping away bridges, it's still there. Fairly rocky in nature, with loose climbs and jagged, technical descents it's a solid technical XC route. However, they say that variety is the spice of life, so the trail also includes fast, smooth and swoopy sections – the end of Slated and the classic Pink Heifer being the prime examples. In a nutshell, the MBR is a cracking ride, with plenty of good, varied singletrack but without the distance of some of the other routes here.

THE TAWR TRAIL

DISTANCE: 20KM	TIME: 1.5–3HRS
EFFORT: 3/5	TECHNICALITY: 3/5

The trail formerly known as the Red Bull has aged well. New sections have been added and others have been removed, but it's still a classic. The old rocky and technical triple-whammy of Snap, Crackle and Pop is still there, but they've been joined by some faster and more flowing sections. The Rocky Horror Show lets you get a fair bit of speed up and the Mantrap rattles downhill over rock slabs. A little quieter than the other trails at Coed y Brenin, the Tarw is also the only completely independent route – making it a good choice for a second ride of the day.

Trails continue…

COED Y BRENIN
continued...

DRAGON'S BACK TRAIL
DISTANCE: 31KM	TIME: 3–5HRS
EFFORT: 4/5	TECHNICALITY: 4/5

THE BEAST OF COED Y BRENIN
DISTANCE: 38KM	TIME: 3–6HRS
EFFORT: 5/5	TECHNICALITY: 4/5

At 31km, it's a large dragon, so make sure you're feeling fit. Another great trail, the Dragon's Back starts out over rock slabs, hits some fast berms and then enters Big Doug – a technical root-and-rock-fest through the rhododendrons. Then comes Herman, with his fast corners and the Addams Family, once seriously tricky characters but now smoothed out to become fast and flowing. You decide if that's a good thing or not. The difficulty then picks up as the trail mixes high speeds with rocks and tight corners before a long uphill drag leads to the rocky finale. Lots of singletrack and lots of distance – lots of fun!

Yet again, Coed y Brenin delivers the goods in combining the MBR and Dragon's Back trails to create The Beast – one of the best trail centre routes around. Covering a fair distance and packing in a lot of high-quality singletrack, it's not easy, but it is unquestionably a trail worth riding. Virtually every singletrack taste is catered for – and in such an enjoyable manner that the route feels a good deal shorter than it actually is. That said, you need to be fit and technically proficient get the most out of it. There's a café halfway round and, with a bit of careful map reading and a willingness to tackle a steep road climb, you can avoid the long forest road drag at the back end of the route…

WIG WORLAND

CWMCARN

About the centre

Cwmcarn's Twrch Trail was one of the first purpose-built mountain bike trails to open in the UK and has remained a firm favourite with many riders. It's seen a few changes here and there, but by and large, it hasn't changed much over the years. Despite being easily accessible (only half an hour's drive from the Severn Crossing and Cardiff) it never seems to get too crowded, so Cwmcarn is always worth a visit. A major asset to Cwmcarn is the Mojo Downhill track, which opened in 2005. Flat-out fast over roots and jumps, its popularity has grown and grown, thanks partly to the superb uplift service that runs there most days of the week. (See *www.cwmdown.co.uk* for details).

Centre pros and cons

+ The Twrch Trail is almost entirely singletrack, with some outstanding sections that you'll remember for a long time
+ There's plenty of technical interest on the climbs and traverses to take your mind off the pedalling
+ The trail throws in a little bit of everything – rocks, roots and silky smooth sections
+ The Cwmdown uplift means the DH course is easily accessible most days of the year
+ Reasonable facilities
− Watch out for the wind up at the freeride area
− Nothing for complete beginners
− Only one XC trail

Directions

From J28 of the M4, head north on the A467, following signs for Cwmcarn Forest Drive. Keep going straight ahead until the fifth roundabout. Turn right and then right at the next roundabout. Cwmcarn Forest Drive is the second turning on your left.

Grid Ref: ST 230936   **Sat Nav:** NP11 7FA

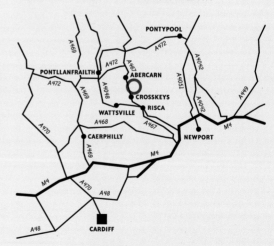

The trails

TWRCH TRAIL	
DISTANCE: 14KM	**TIME:** 1–2HRS
TECHNICALITY: 3/5	**EFFORT:** 3/5

Winding up alongside the river, over fiddly rocky sections and sharp little climbs, the Twrch Trail starts as it means to continue. Swinging uphill, you'd better be feeling determined or the tough climb with its steep pitches and rooty obstacles will have you dabbing a foot. Once up, take a breather and bounce around the tight corners of the fantastic Airstream, spiral through the woods towards a couple of faster, rougher sections, and then climb to some fast, swooping woodland riding. Rattle out across an exposed traverse and the blast down the final shallow berms and jumps as fast as you dare. Then go around again.

MOJO DOWNHILL	
DISTANCE: 1.7–1.9KM	**TIME:** 5–10 MINS
EFFORT: 5/5	**TECHNICALITY:** 4/5

The Mojo Downhill has two runs: an easier red and a more technical black, both of which contain plenty of roots, turns and jumps. Neither is particularly technical for a downhill run, meaning they are rideable by relative beginners, while becoming scorchingly fast for better riders. The runs converge towards the bottom of the hill to share a lower section which is flat out over big jumps and around massive berms – worth pushing up for even if you don't bother going all the way to the top.

Freeride

The Freeride is an optional section at the top of the XC loop. It's got three ladder drops of varying heights, a corkscrew into a tunnel, a row of table tops and a massive wall ride.

Good to know

You'll need to book in advance for the Cwmdown uplift. Currently, the service runs Wednesday to Sunday. See *www.cwmdown.co.uk* for details.

PHIL LEWIS

CWM RHAEADR

About the centre

As purpose-built trail centres go, Cwm Rhaeadr is a bit of an odd one. There's only one trail, no facilities and it's only 6km long. It's also pretty much in the middle of nowhere. Opened in 2006, the trail was designed and built by Rowan Sorrell and is, essentially, a mini version of the nearby Brechfa Gorlech trail he created. This means you can expect a well-surfaced trail with a lot of jumps, berms and compressions. Although the trail here is short, it's entertaining enough for a few laps and could easily be combined with a trip to Brechfa, Afan or the Brecon Beacons.

Centre pros and cons

+ Great fun for those who like to pump and jump their way downhill
+ All weather venue, if a tiny bit exposed at the top.
− At 6km, it's a short trail
− No facilities and rather tucked away in the middle of nowhere

Directions

From Llandovery, take the A40 heading south west towards Llandeilo. After half a mile, cross the river and take the first right, onto a minor road. Follow this towards the small village of Cilycwm. Go straight through the village on the same road until you reach the car park for the trail on your left after about 2 miles.

Grid Ref: SN 765422   **Sat Nav:** SA20 0TL

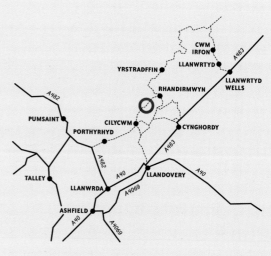

The trail

DISTANCE: 6KM	TIME: 0.5–1HR
EFFORT: 2/5	TECHNICALITY: 3/5

This trail is about enjoying descending. That means that the ride begins with a big forest-road climb – the aim is to get you to the top in the fastest and easiest way possible. That said, it's pleasant enough thanks to the nice views higher up the trail. Towards the top, the forest road gives way to some loose singletrack, which continues to climb steeply in places, but is relatively painless. Then comes the descent, which is essentially a big BMX track through the woods. It's a little loose, but is fast and full of jumps and berms and compressions. It flows so well that you can pump your way down the whole descent almost as fast as you can ride it pedalling. Great fun!

JOHN COEFIELD

HAMISH McCOOL

GWYDYR FOREST

About the centre

Another trail opened relatively early in trail centre history, the Marin Trail in Gwydyr Forest mixes singletrack descents with forest road climbs. In doing so, it seems to be falling in riders' estimation as more modern trails are developed, which is a shame, as it's a fine trail. The singletrack is fast and flowing, rather than technical, making this an enjoyable trail for a range of riders – it's easy to ride, but a lot of fun when taken at speed. Sitting in the woods above Betws-y-Coed, it's in a great location too. There's plenty more to do nearby and you're never far from the shops, restaurants and accommodation available in Betws, which makes it a good base for a trip.

Centre pros and cons

+ A fantastic, fast, jumpy and swoopy final descent
+ Great location – Betws-y-Coed has full facilities and, being bang in the middle of Snowdonia, there's a mass of other riding/walking/climbing to be had
+ The relatively technically straightforward trail makes this a good choice for a range of riders
− Lots of forest road climbing
− Nothing for complete beginners

Directions

Turn off the main road (the A5) through Betws-y-Coed beside the chip shop in the centre of town. Cross the bridge and follow the road around to the right. Continue straight ahead for about 3.5 miles (6km) until you pass Gwydir Castle on your right. Just after this, turn left up a minor road. The car park is on your left. If you reach a T-junction, you've gone slightly too far.

Grid Ref: SH 790610   **Sat Nav:** LL26 0PN

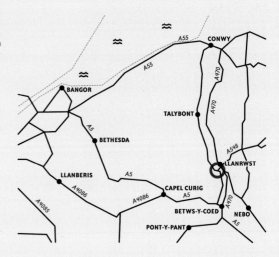

The trails

MARIN TRAIL	
DISTANCE: 25KM	**TIME:** 1–2.5HRS
EFFORT: 3/5	**TECHNICALITY:** 3/5

With a big b*gger of a climb straight out of the car park and a fair amount of forest road climbing along its length, the Marin Trail doesn't sound like a promising option. But, throw in fast, twisting trails, pleasant open singletrack and a jagged rocky section – as well as some of the best views of any trail centre (out over Snowdonia – complete with benches to admire them from) and things are looking up. The clincher may be the final few stretches of singletrack descent. Long, winding and as fast as you like with some large humps and compressions giving plenty of opportunities to take to the air, it's a great way to finish the ride on a high.

Good to know

- You can ride to the trail from the town. Cross the bridge by the chip shop and turn left past the car park. Climb the road for what seems like an eternity (about 2km), keeping an eye out for the route – it crosses the road you're on after a particularly steep stretch of tarmac.
- You're also only a short distance from Penmachno – why not ride one trail in the morning and the other later in the day?

FORESTRY COMMISSION PICTURE LIBRARY / ISOBEL CAMERON

FORESTRY COMMISSION PICTURE LIBRARY / ISOBEL CAMERON

MACH TRAILS

About the centre

The seat of the Welsh Parliament in the 15th Century, Machynlleth is a lively town with a decent range of places to stay, to eat and to ride. Thanks to Dyfi Mountain Biking, a local group of riders and businesses, it also now contains the Mach Trails. These are three waymarked routes, varying in length, which explore the countryside to the south of Machynlleth. Following bridleways, forest roads and quiet lanes, there's no singletrack and little technical difficulty – these are trails for getting out and about and enjoying the countryside.

Centre pros and cons

+ The Mach Trails are a great way of getting out into 'proper' countryside without having to worry about planning a route
+ The countryside around Machynlleth is beautiful – there are some great views and you'll pass through some very pleasant woodland
+ The routes are great if you're after a nice day out on easy terrain – but watch out for 'The Chute'
+ Although it's the only technical section on the marked routes, The Chute is a quite an entertaining finish
- You'll need to pick up a route leaflet from The Holy Trail and take a map with you – the waymarks can be easy to miss
- These aren't the trails to pick if you're after singletrack or technical challenges

Directions

Machynlleth sits on a T-junction between the A487, which runs between Aberystwyth and Dolgellau, and the A489 which comes in from the east.

Grid Ref: SH 746008   **Sat Nav:** SY20 8EB

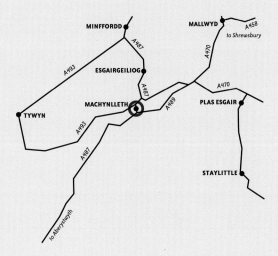

The trails

MACH 1

DISTANCE: 16KM	TIME: 1.5–3HRS
EFFORT: 3/5	TECHNICALITY: 2/5

It may be the shortest route here, but it's no pushover. Starting out along a cycle path adjacent to the main road south from Machynlleth, the Mach 1 contains some long, steep climbs. Luckily, they are all on reasonable surfaces and in pleasant surroundings, so each one is rideable and there's always something to look at. Speaking of surroundings, part of the ride runs beside a deep gorge with a river at its base and some water-filled caves beside the track. There are no particularly technical sections on the ride and many of the descents are on tarmac. A pleasant ride, well within the capabilities of most mountain bikers.

MACH 2

DISTANCE: 24 KM	TIME: 2–4HRS
EFFORT: 4/5	TECHNICALITY: 2/5

Passing through open fields, up forest tracks and between gorse bushes, the Mach 2 passes through some varied terrain. This means there's a lot to see, you're constantly riding over different surfaces and the feel of the ride changes with each passing mile. Unfortunately, the majority of the route's descents are, as with the Mach 1, on tarmac, and the loose stone, rocky slabs and loamy ground is left for climbing. Still, it's probably the most enjoyable ride here and there is some good riding to be had, especially in the final quarter of the route as the trail narrows to a grassy track through fields of sheep.

MACH 3

DISTANCE: 30KM	TIME: 3–6HRS
EFFORT: 5/5	TECHNICALITY: 3/5

At 30 kilometres, the Mach 3 is a relatively long route. Climbing to nearly 500 metres, it's the hilliest here and, careering down 'The Chute', it's also the most technical. For the most part, the trail follows quiet lanes and easy forest tracks which carry you high up into the hills for some great views. There's some decent riding: grassy bridleways and fast, if easy, descents to provide some entertainment. Don't forget the aforementioned Chute, a tricky, rocky descent. You'll need some good descent skills for this, and a fair degree of fitness for the remainder of the route. A nice day out in the country.

Good to know

- You'll need a map as the waymarking signs are small and easy to miss. Pick up OS Explorer 215.
- You'll also need to have a rough idea of where the routes go – either pick up a leaflet in The Holey Trail or visit the Dyfi Mountain Biking website.
- Some of the routes pass through working forests, which can be closed. Ask in town first.

Finding the trails from Machynlleth:

- Mach 1 – From the centre of Machynlleth, head south along the A487 towards Aberystwyth. After about 4km, turn left in the small village of Derwnelas, picking up waymarks as you do so.
- Machs 2 and 3 – Head along the A489 from the centre of town (towards Penegoes) until you spot Forge Road on your right. Head along this into Forge and fork right, where you'll pick up waymarks.

NANT YR ARIAN

About the centre

High up in the hills above Aberystwyth, Nant yr Arian's trails are some of the finest in Wales. Known for its long singletrack runs, the big climb in the middle of the Summit Trail, the big, wilderness Syfydrin Loop and the Red Kites that swoop around the car park, it's a centre worth visiting. There's not much for complete beginners, and there aren't many chances to get your wheels in the air, but it's hard to argue with the miles of smooth, flowing singletrack on offer.

Centre pros and cons

+ Good for XC riding – lots of fast, swooping singletrack
+ The singletrack varies from fast, open trails to hillside traverses and tight stuff in the trees
+ Takes in some more natural riding – wide, rocky climbs and descents that require a bit of line choice
+ The Syfydrin Trail offers a big trip out into the hills
+ Reasonable facilities
− The car park and visitor centre can get busy – but luckily not just with riders
− There's a never-ending climb part way round – but what goes up…

Directions

From Aberystwyth, take the A44 east towards Rhayader. The centre is on your left after around 10 miles (16 km).
Grid Ref: SN 718813   **Sat Nav:** SY23 3AD

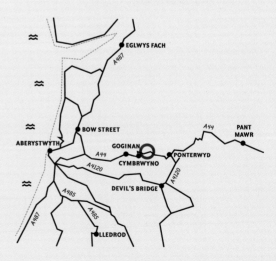

The trails

PENDAM TRAIL

DISTANCE: 9KM	TIME: 1–2HRS
EFFORT: 3/5	TECHNICALITY: 3/5

A bite-sized version of the Summit Trail, the Pendam is the one to ride when you're short on time. Flying down the initial fast, open singletrack, you're quickly up to speed and leaning through the corners. A short section of forest road and you're into the trees, carving around berms before a stiff climb (luckily only the top quarter of the main Summit climb) carries you up for the final, High as a Kite descent. Here things tighten and roughen up for a soaring descent through the trees to the final twisting corners and the visitor centre. Not too tricky and not too long, this is another trail that can be enjoyed by a wide range of riders.

SUMMIT TRAIL

DISTANCE: 16KM	TIME: 1.5–3HRS
EFFORT: 3/5	TECHNICALITY: 3/5

The Summit Trail is the backbone of Nant yr Arian. It's the trail that packs in the most singletrack, creating a fast, flowing ride. Open in places and snaking through the trees in others, the trail is never too technical, leaving you to concentrate on the corners and take them as fast, or as slow as you like. It's a good formula – there are fast, loose corners, tight corners around trees and just about everything in between. The singletrack sections are all long (as is the never-ending climb in the middle of the route), which really allows you to get into the swing of things and enjoy your riding. Another cracking Welsh route.

SYFYDRIN TRAIL

DISTANCE: 35KM	TIME: 3–5HRS
EFFORT: 4/5	TECHNICALITY: 3/5

The Syfydrin branches off the Summit Trail to carve a big loop with a really 'out there' feel through the surrounding countryside. It's not particularly technical, but it's rocky enough to spice up the climbs and descents, and there are some great views before the trail swings back onto the fantastic singletrack of the Summit Trail. So it's a long ride with some good singletrack and some solid natural riding.

JAMES DYMOND

PENMACHNO

AT A GLANCE

BEGINNERS: 2/3   **INTERMEDIATE:** 3/3   **ADVANCED:** 2/3

FACILITIES

THE TRAILS

Loop 1 .... Red 20km
Loop 2 .... Red 10km

NEAREST BIKE SHOP

Beics Betws, Betws-y-Coed – t: 01690 710 766

MORE INFORMATION

w: www.mbwales.com   w: www.bikewales.co.uk

About the centre

'Loop 1' and 'Loop 2'... not the most imaginative or sparklingly witty of trail names, but undeniably accurate and impossible to argue with. And that's pretty much the same for the riding. There are no unique trail features here, no jumps, and no rock gardens – just good, solid singletrack. It's for this reason that many riders rate it as their favourite trail centre. The no frills approach extends to the facilities – there are none. This is because the centre was developed as part of a community project, led by the voluntary group Menter Bro Machno and all the money raised has gone into the construction of the trails. Still, there's a pub in Penmachno and Betws-y-Coed is just up the road, so it's hardly a problem.

Centre pros and cons

+ Apart from a couple of sections near the start, the route is almost entirely singletrack
+ The last couple of descents are fast, rocky masterpieces
+ The routes are technically easy enough for fit but inexperienced riders, but still a lot of fun if you like to ride fast
– No facilities
– The trail is exposed in places, so dress sensibly on wet and windy days

Directions

From Betws-y-Coed, head east on the A5. Once over the bridge and out of the town, take the second right, onto the B4406, signed to Penmachno. Follow the road into, and through Penmachno. The trail begins from a small car park on your right, about half a mile (1km) from the last house.

Grid Ref: SH 786498   **Sat Nav:** PENMACHNO

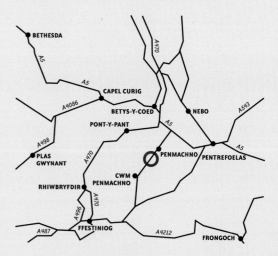

The trails

LOOP 1	
DISTANCE: 20KM	**TIME:** 1.5–3HRS
EFFORT: 3/5	**TECHNICALITY:** 3/5

Riding Penmachno is like compiling a medley of all your favourite songs and listening to them back to back. Each track is good, it all feels reassuringly familiar and you just know you'll enjoy it. This is an unashamedly XC trail – there are no massively bermed or jumpy sections – just tight, flowing singletrack. It's never too technical (the roots and awkward rocks have been smoothed out), meaning you can concentrate on the corners and compressions that weave through the woods. Each piece of singletrack rides well and blends into the sections before and after it – always a good sign. It's the final descent, however, that makes the trail. It's fast, it's rocky and it goes on and on and on. A great way to ensure that you finish the ride on a high!

LOOP 2	
DISTANCE: 10 KM	**TIME:** 1–1.5HRS
EFFORT: 3/5	**TECHNICALITY:** 3/5

Loop 2 is an extension to… er… Loop 1. By taking it, you miss out on a couple of hundred metres of forest road climbing and gain a good deal of decent singletrack. Fairly flat in nature, there are no big climbs or descents – so you end up doing a lot of pedalling to keep your speed. The singletrack is good – not too technical, but nice and flowing with the odd tricky section here and there. You never seem to spend more than a couple of minutes on forest road between sections and there are some great views. A worthwhile addition to Loop 1. The downsides? It can get exposed in bad weather, and I was once beaten down a section of a singletrack by a particularly swift sheep.

Good to know

Drop some money in the honesty box – you'll help to repair the trails and improve what's already there.

📷 DAN BARHAM

TOP 10:
Tricky Trails

Think you can clean any manmade trail? After all, it's all been built to be ridden, right? And you are good, aren't you?

1 Stainburn
Brilliantly hard. A ridiculous black, tricky XC and fast red make this the most technically challenging trail centre in the UK.

2 Golspie's black
Tricky, rocky climbing leads to a descent packed with rocks, drops and jumps. Great fun.

3 Learnie's black
Home of the steep rocky staircase (with corners).

4 Laggan's black
Unrelenting. Rock obstacle follows rock obstacle.

5 Mabie's Kona Dark Side
How's your balance? Not too high, scary, full of jumps, this is some of the most technical north shore in the country.

6 Drumlanrig's Hell's Cauldron
How do you like roots?

7 Llandegla's black
Easy enough to roll, the speeds achievable on this bermed trail are scarily high.

8 Innerleithen's Traquair XC (the black bits)
You need a full range of riding skills to get the most out of Plora Craig and Caddon Bank.

9 Balblair
Natural trails over granite slabs and down steep descents. Tricky XC riding at its best.

10 Coed y Brenin's Beast
Pretty straightforward if you're good – this is the home of technical XC.

KONA DARK SIDE, MABIE TIM RUSSON

SECTION
BIKE PARKS

4

If singletrack riding isn't really your thing, or you'd like to dip your toes in more extreme waters, try visiting one of the many bike parks dotted across the country. Varying from full-on downhill venues to north shore and jump spots, they encourage a very different style of riding to the XC trails. In no way is this any more than a cursory look at such spots and we've only included the largest, public centres. They are graded according to their suitability for riders from different disciplines.

Important: The *Beginners/Intermediate/Advanced* rating assumes a high level of riding skill. Beginners here would be capable of riding trails graded black and orange by the Forestry Commission and be looking to advance their skills.

BALNAIN

AT A GLANCE
BEGINNERS: 2/3   INTERMEDIATE: 2/3   ADVANCED: 2/3

FACILITIES
(P)

THE TRAILS
Downhill 0/3
4X 0/3
North Shore 2/3
Jumping 2/3

MORE INFORMATION
w: www.10glens.co.uk

HOWARD COTTON

What's there?

Balnain focuses on woodwork. There's a tricky trials-oriented
area that is not easy, thanks to some very skinny sections,
tight turns and hops between rocks. Then there's an extensive,
although far easier, north shore section. It's not too narrow and
doesn't have any drops or gaps, but is good fun all the same.
Beside this is a more limited jump area, with a gap or two and
a couple of short, bermed runs leading into a jump box.
You can jump onto and drop off this, or wallride the sloping
sides. There's also a 'beginners' area with a couple of obstacles
and some low, moveable north shore if you're just starting out.

Directions

From Inverness, take the A82 south towards Fort William.
After 14 miles, turn right in Drumnadrochit onto the A831.
The car park is 4 miles up the road on your right.
Grid Ref: NH 449298   **Sat Nav:** BALNAIN

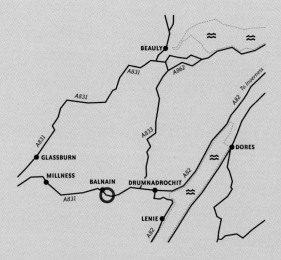

BLANDFORD FORUM
UK Bike Park

AT A GLANCE

BEGINNERS: 2/3 **INTERMEDIATE:** 2/3 **ADVANCED:** 3/3

FACILITIES

Ⓟ ⬆

THE TRAILS

Downhill 3/3
4X 3/3
North Shore 2/3
Jumping 2/3

NEAREST BIKE SHOP

Torico Bike Shop – **t:** 01258 473 770

MORE INFORMATION

w: www.ukbikepark.com

Directions

From Blandford Forum (on the A354 between Salisbury and Dorchester), take the A350 north towards Shaftesbury before turning left onto the A357 towards Sturminster Newington. Torico bike shop is in a small industrial estate on the far side of Sturminster Newington, if you need to buy a permit. Continue to the village of Shillingstone and turn left opposite the church, towards Okeford Fitzpaine. In the village, turn left at the T-junction and then bear left when the road forks. Parking is on your left at the top of the hill and the park is along the track on the other side of the road.

Grid Ref: ST 817093   **Sat Nav:** SHILLINGSTONE

What's there?

Go to Blandford if you're in the south and want to ride downhill. There are several runs to choose from, all twisting and turning down a steep bowl in the woods. There are roots and trees aplenty, several drops of varying height and a fair few jumps. The runs vary in difficulty, but are all worth riding. There's a regular uplift service and the hill is a popular race venue. At the top you will find a 4X course and a few short sections of north shore, where the emphasis is on big gaps and drops. A good venue with a lot to offer. If you're planning a visit, you need to buy a permit. These are available from Torico bike shop in nearby Shillingstone – see the website for more details.

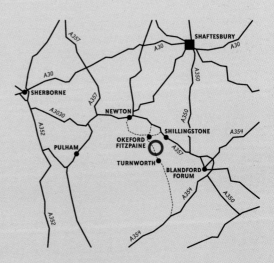

ESHER

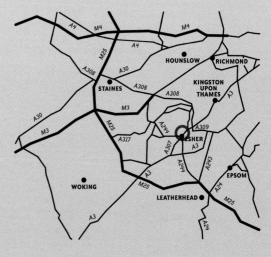

📷 © MBR (MOUNTAIN BIKE RIDER) MAGAZINE

What's there?

Esher is a pretty unique place. The first thing you see on arrival is the small 'slopestyle' area by the car park, which boasts some nicely crafted jumps. Carry on around the corner, however, and you find the north shore that Esher is famous for. Due to various health and safety regulations, there's nothing massively high, and certainly nothing high and skinny. That's not to say it's boring, or not hard though! There's plenty of narrow, technical stuff low to the ground (watch out for your disk rotors) and a LOT of gaps and jumps – some of which are pretty technical while others are just big. Esher is one of a kind and well worth a visit.

Directions

Leave the M25 at Junction 10 and head into London on the A3. After 4 miles, turn left at onto the A244, following signs for Esher. After 2 miles, continue across Esher High Street at the traffic lights and go straight on, towards the war memorial. Go straight on to the right (passing the memorial on your left) and turn right into Sandown Racecourse, following signs for the Leisure Centre. Turn right again and follow signs.

Grid Ref: TQ 140650   **Sat Nav:** KT10 8AN

PENSHURST
P.O.R.C.

AT A GLANCE

BEGINNERS: 2/3   **INTERMEDIATE:** 2/3   **ADVANCED:** 2/3

FACILITIES

THE TRAILS

Downhill 2/3
4X 3/3
North Shore 1/3
Jumping 3/3

MORE INFORMATION

w: www.ukdirt.com/porc
P.O.R.C. – t: 01892 870 136

Directions

From Tonbridge, take the A26 south west towards Royal Tunbridge Wells. Turn right shortly after crossing the A21, onto the B2176, following signs to Penshurst. Follow the road into the village and turn left, just after the pub, onto Fordcombe Road (B2188). Cross the river and turn right up Grove Road. P.O.R.C. is up a small track on your left towards the top of the hill.

Grid Ref: TQ 516427   **Sat Nav:** TN11 8DU

What's there?

Penshurst Off Road Cycling (P.O.R.C) is a strange place. Set on the side of a hill, there's a pretty decent set of dirt jumps at the top, a massive 4X course, along which you can reach speeds that can only be accurately described as 'silly' and just below them a rather limited XC loop off the back. Other than that, the hill is covered in berms, gaps and drops that can be linked in numerous ways to form various downhill runs. Some are tight, some are pretty big and some are fast. They are all rutted and worn, upping the technicality dramatically. They are all fairly short (this is Kent, after all) but good fun. A good venue – there's a lot there and there's always something new being built.

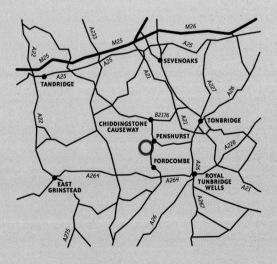

If you enjoy bike park riding and want more, you could do worse than check out the following centres, which have received full listings earlier in this guide.

Aston Hill – see page 24

BEGINNERS: 2/3   **INTERMEDIATE:** 3/3   **ADVANCED:** 2/3

Downhill 3/3
4X 3/3
North Shore 0/3
Jumping 0/3

What's there?

Another regular venue on the Southern Downhill and 4X scenes, Aston Hill caters well for both riding disciplines. There are four downhill runs, varying from the relatively smooth and straightforward to the highly technical and exciting. What they all share is a rooty, chalky nature, making them pretty slick and tricky in the wet, and they all drop steeply down through the trees. They are also all, unsurprisingly, a right laugh! If you'd rather ride 4X, head for the top of the hill, where the relatively short track offers a range of jumps and a couple of big berms.

Chicksands – see page 30

BEGINNERS: 2/3   **INTERMEDIATE:** 3/3   **ADVANCED:** 3/3

Downhill 1/3
4X 3/3
North Shore 3/3
Jumping 3/3

What's there?

Chicksands' extremely popular bike park is highly regarded – with good reason. One of the best venues in the south of England for jumping and north shore, it's got a decent 4X course, a couple of sets of dirt jumps and a load of drops of various shapes and sizes – plenty to go at. If you prefer riding woodwork, there's the 'Chick Shore' area, with its gap jumps, drops and technical north shore. You need to pay to use this area at weekends and on bank holidays (see *www.chicksandsbikepark.co.uk* for more information) but it's still definitely worth a visit if you're anywhere near the area.

Glentress & Innerleithen – see pages 120 & 128

BEGINNERS: 3/3   **INTERMEDIATE:** 3/3   **ADVANCED:** 3/3

Downhill 3/3
4X 0/3
North Shore 2/3
Jumping 2/3

What's there?

Glentress's bike park is worth riding whether you're a beginner or a decent bike-handler. With several lines of jumps of varying difficulty, north shore, wall rides and a jump box, there's plenty for everybody to go at. If you'd rather ride downhill than jumps, head a little way down the road to Innerleithen. It's is one of the UK's premier downhill venues, featuring everything from high-speed runs over jumps and drops to more intricate courses for those who prefer their riding to be tight and technical. There's a regular uplift if you need it as well. The Tweed Valley does get busy, but that's a testament to just how good it is.

Mabie – see page 146

BEGINNERS: 1/3   **INTERMEDIATE:** 2/3   **ADVANCED:** 3/3

Downhill 0/3
4X 1/3
North Shore 3/3
Jumping 1/3

What's there?

Although definitely an XC venue and in no way a bike park, Mabie's infamous Dark Side and Mini-X courses make it worth highlighting. The Mini-X course is essentially a short 4X course. Pretty good fun, but probably not worth making a special trip for – but the Dark Side is! It is undoubtedly the most technical north shore at any major trail centre. Unlike Esher, there are no big drops and only one (avoidable) gap. Instead, Mabie is like an XC north shore trail. It's long, continuous and unrelentingly technical, with tyre-width skinnies leading to impossibly-tight corners and tricky rock gardens. Absolutely brilliant.

GLENTRESS BIKE PARK 📷 WIG WORLAND

WHAT GOES INTO BUILDING
A PURPOSE-BUILT MTB TRAIL?

Well before riders have the chance to ride a finished trail, or even before the first spade goes into the ground, a great deal of behind-the-scenes work takes place. Site visits, pre-start paperwork, risk assessments, method statements and emergency planning all form part of these first steps. It's also important for the project team to meet, including the trail designer and engineer. Once the green light has been given, the first few days on site involve setting up the compound, meeting the lorries that move equipment from the previous project and taking delivery of materials such as timberwork and drainage pipes.

Attention can then turn to building the trail, which begins with *macro* setting out of the trail corridor for each section of trail. This is the foundation or footprint of the trail – the big picture – and from this we can see how the trail will flow, where the climbs and descents will be, where natural features already exist that can be incorporated into the trail and consider the trail's sustainability. As contractors this is sometimes done prior to getting to site or it might be the first stage of the contract.

The next step is the *micro* setting out. This dictates the exact line of the trail and is the stage in which all the berms, turns, rocks and drops are planned and crafted into the final trail. The micro setting out is done on a day-to-day basis as the excavator and trail finisher move along the trail corridor. We strive to achieve a natural organic feel to the trail surface by using materials found within the trail corridor whenever possible.

We use a 5-ton zero tail swing excavator (digger) on our singletrack trails, as this gives us the maximum power/footprint ratio. The excavators are fitted with an *'encon'* tilt/rotator bucket – this nifty bucket makes for the ultimate in shaping and sculpting of the trail and trail verges. After the excavator has done its stuff, the trail finisher takes over, checking the trails and angles, tweaking the turns and lots and lots of compaction with a whacker plate. Finally, we move on to the *dressing up* of the trail, which is the placing of key objects at the side of the trail such as rocks, logs, vegetation or stumps, and gardening and tidying of the trail verges.

Only now do we ride the trail – to make sure it works the way it was designed to. Then we ride it again and again and again and again… At this point the trails are slow, sticky and slippery, but with the natural process of weathering, the trail 'seals and heals', and just gets better and better.

Why dress up a trail? All new trails look very raw when newly constructed and it's hard to distinguish the trail from the verge when riding at speed, so we dress the trail with natural objects from within the trail corridor to give the rider focus when riding, such as those logs that just stopped you cutting that corner. The trail soon becomes a defined line and the vegetation begins to grow on the trail verge. The trail will eventually become a single ribbon, threading through a natural green corridor. That's what we aim for; it just takes a little time and co-operation with nature to deliver the final package.

Hugh Clixby
Clixbys Trailbuilders

WHINLATTER 📷 JOHN COEFIELD

Glossary

Berm A banked corner, allowing the rider to carry a lot of speed through a turn.

Compression A dip in the trail. Useful for pumping (see below).

Chicken Run An alternative, easier line around a tricky or scary section of trail.

Double A jump consisting of two mounds of earth which are jumped between. A tabletop (see below) with the middle removed.

Drop off/Drop Anything where the ground drops away suddenly. Sometimes rollable, sometimes not – you might need to get airborne to clear them safely.

Gap jump Pretty self-explanatory! Don't under-jump...

North Shore/ Boardwalk Trails built from wooden slats and usually raised off the ground. The term originated in Canada, where such constructions were used to cross wet or boggy ground. Often easily rideable, but can be made narrow, high and technically difficult.

Off-camber A trail that slopes from one side to the other, in exactly the direction you don't want it to!

Pump 'Pumping' a trail involves pushing the bike down slopes and into compressions, and making it as light as possible for short rises, in order to gain 'free' speed from the trail.

Rock garden A section of trail dominated by rocks.

Singletrack A trail only wide enough for one bike, forcing the rider to follow the trail's twists and turns. Brilliant!

Switchback A corner that doubles back on itself in a 'U' shape.

Tabletop A jump with a flat top between the take off and landing ramps, allowing the jump to be rolled and reducing the likelihood of crashing in the event of under-jumping.

XC/Cross Country Riding around, uphill and downhill, generally enjoying being out on your bike! The sort of riding that everybody does from time to time.

Useful Websites

Mountain Biking Trails

www.**ukmountainbiking**.co.uk
www.**imba**.org.uk
www.**forestry**.gov.uk
www.**mbwales**.com
www.**mtb-wales**.com
www.**mtbwales**.co.uk
www.**7stanes**.gov.uk
www.**scottishmountainbike**.com
cycling.**visitscotland**.com

Mountain Biking News and General

www.**v-outdoor**.co.uk
www.**mbr**.co.uk
www.**singletrackworld**.com
www.**bikemagic**.com
www.**shecycles**.com
www.**bikeradar**.com

Get Involved

www.**singletraction**.org.uk
www.**wharncliffe**.info
www.**gorrick**.com/**swinley**

Weather

www.**meto**.gov.uk
www.**metcheck**.com
www.**bbc**.co.uk/**weather**

Accommodation

Unfortunately, there's no room in this guide for a detailed list of accommodation. If there's accommodation at a trail centre, it's been included in that centre's listing. If you're in a popular tourist area like North Wales, accommodation is easy – there are campsites, hotels and B&Bs everywhere. If you want to camp, grab a detailed map and look out for sites. Otherwise, try the local Tourist Information Centre (see below) or some of the websites listed above and below.

www.**hostel-scotland**.co.uk .... Scottish independent hostels
www.**syha**.org.uk .... Scottish Youth Hostel Association
www.**visittweedvalley**.co.uk .... Portal to the Tweed Valley
www.**yha**.org.uk .... Youth Hostel Association
www.**touristinformationcentres**.com . Find your closest TIC
www.**thecyclepeople**.com .... Database of accommodation
www.**visitwales**.com ..... Database of Welsh accommodation
www.**visitbritain**.co.uk .... Another searchable database
www.**enjoyengland**.com .... Info on campsites
www.**camping.uk-directory**.com .... Info on campsites
www.**find-a-campsite**.co.uk .... Info on campsites
www.**ukcampsite**.co.uk .... Info on campsites

FOR INFORMATION ABOUT TRAIL CENTRE UPDATES AND TO DOWNLOAD SATNAV POINT OF INTEREST FILES FOR FREE, VISIT: WWW.UKMOUNTAINBIKING.CO.UK

MOUNTAIN BIKING GUIDEBOOKS

VERTEBRATE PUBLISHING

The Guidebooks

Each guidebook features up to 28 rides, complete with comprehensive directions, specialist mapping and inspiring photography, all in a pocket-sized, portable format. The routes are also available on CD, with each route set up in PDF format to allow you to print off just the route you're going to ride and leave the book at home or in the car. Written by riders for riders, our guides are designed to maximise ride-ability and are full of useful local area information.

About the Great Outdoors

The great outdoors is not bottom bracket friendly; beautiful flowing singletrack can give way suddenly to scary rock gardens, hard climbs can appear right at the end of a ride and sheep will laugh at your attempts to clean your nemesis descent. Of course it's not all good news. You'll need a good bike to ride many of the routes in our set of mountain biking guides. You'll also need fuel, spare clothing, first aid skills, endurance, power, determination and plenty of nerve.

Bridleways litter our great outdoors. Our guides, written by local riders, reveal the secrets of their local area's best rides from 10 to 100km in length, including ideas for link-ups and night-riding options. Critically acclaimed, our comprehensive series of guides is the country's bestselling and most respected – purpose-built for the modern mountain biker.